KARL MARX

[*Photo: The British Museum.*

KARL MARX

KARL
MARX

By
KARL KORSCH

New York
RUSSELL & RUSSELL
1963

FIRST PUBLISHED IN 1938
REISSUED, 1963, BY RUSSELL & RUSSELL, INC.
BY ARRANGEMENT WITH CHAPMAN & HALL, LTD. LONDON
L. C. CATALOG CARD NO: 63—15166
PRINTED IN THE UNITED STATES OF AMERICA

21518

CONTENTS

CONTENTS

INTRODUCTION

K ARL MARX was born in Trier in 1818 and died as a
political exile in London, 1883. When he had completed
his studies at the Universities of Bonn and Berlin, and served his
first political apprenticeship as an editor of the *Rheinische Zeitung*
in Cologne, 1842-43, he found himself cut off from almost every
link with his native country. His father had died in 1838, he had
"fallen out with his family" since 1842, and all the plans for his
future had collapsed under the blows of the Christian-Romantic
reaction which set in with the accession of King Frederick
William IV in 1840. "In Germany there is now nothing I can
do," Marx wrote to Ruge in January 1843. "In Germany one
can only be false to oneself." Thus, in the autumn of 1843, after
marrying the woman he had wooed for seven years, he went to
Paris and, when expelled from France in 1845, turned to Belgium
where he stayed until the revolution of 1848 made possible a
short return to political activity in his own country, as an editor
of the *Neue Rheinische Zeitung*, 1848-49. After that, expelled
from Germany, France, Belgium, he spent the remaining three
decades of his life in the great refuge of revolutionary exiles from
all European countries which in those times was London. He
tried in vain to earn a living for his growing family by journal-
istic work and was saved from starvation only by the untiring
services of his life-long friend and collaborator, Friedrich Engels,
who devoted the next eighteen years of his life to the hateful
drudgery of "doggish commerce," mainly to help his friend to
complete his great scientific work, *Capital*. When finally he was
able to retire from business with enough money to secure freedom from financial worries both for himself and Marx, it was

9

almost too late. Though the main results of Marx's ever widening and deepening studies had taken final shape in the first volume published in 1867, the remaining parts of *Capital* were never completed. The incessant struggles and miseries inseparable from the life of an inflexible political emigrant had by 1873 finally worn out even that tremendous mental productivity which had been embodied in Marx, although he went on for a further decade to pile up excerpts and notes for the future completion of his work and now and then displayed the full vigour of the old days in such fully matured pieces of workmanship as the Marginal Notes to the Gotha programme of the German workers' party in 1875 and the recently published critical notes on the economic work of Adolf Wagner dated 1881-82.

Nor must we forget what Engels most aptly said at the funeral of his friend in 1883, that the man of science was "not even half the man," but that this man Marx was "above all a revolutionary." Of his two outstanding works, the *Communist Manifesto* and *Capital*, the one was published at the eve of the revolution of 1848 as the working programme of the first international party of the militant vanguard of the proletariat. The other coincided with the beginning of the recovery of western Europe from that protracted depression and stagnation of all progressive forces which had followed upon the bloody defeat of the insurrectionary workers of Paris in June 1848 and the ensuing failure of the European revolution of 1848-50—a period most clearly characterized by the anti-democratic and anti-socialistic totalitarian régime of the third Napoleon in France 1850-70. Marx's theoretical exposition of the bourgeois world in *Capital* coincided, moreover, with his actual participation in the first open and comprehensive experiment in working-class unity, the *International Working Men's Association* inaugurated in 1864. Thus Marx's revolutionary theory and practice formed at all times an inseparable whole, and this whole is what is living to-day of Marx. His real aim, even in this strictly theoretical work, was to co-operate in one way or another in the historical struggle of the modern proletariat, to whom he was the first to give a scientific knowledge of its class position and its class needs, a true and materialistic knowledge of the conditions necessary for its own emancipation and thus, at the same time, for the further development of the social life of mankind.

It is the purpose of this book to restate the most important principles and contents of Marx's social science in the light of recent historical events and of the new theoretical needs which have arisen under the impact of those events. In so doing we shall deal throughout with the original ideas of Marx himself rather than with their subsequent developments brought about by the various "orthodox" and "revisionist," dogmatic and critical, radical and moderate schools of the Marxists on the one hand, and their more or less violent critics and opponents on the other hand. There is to-day a struggle about Marx carried on in practically all countries of the civilized world—from Soviet Russia where Marxism has become the official philosophy of the State, to the Fascist and semi-Fascist countries of central and southern Europe, South America, and Eastern Asia, where they are at present prosecuted and exterminated. Between those two extremes there lies the land of the as yet undecided fight between the so-called "Marxist" and so-called "anti-Marxist" ideas, and thus the only part of the world where it is still possible to-day to discuss with relative freedom the true significance of those genuine principles of Marx which in the meantime have been adapted by friends and foes to an astonishing variety of political purposes which appear from the review of the various historical phases of the Marxist thought. There are more problems involved in this apparent cleavage between the Marxian ideology and its historical realization than can be tackled in a small book. The reader is referred in this respect to the author's previous writings on the subject quoted in the bibliography annexed to this book.

To increase the utility of this presentation of the Marxian theory an attempt has been made to keep the single chapters as far as possible independent. Thus a reader not acquainted with the daring abstractions of classical economic science, may leap over the somewhat difficult second chapter of the first part and read it later in connection with the second part, while a philosophically unprepared reader might reserve the highly general statements of II, 4, on the development of Marx from Philosophy to Science until he has studied the same problem in the more specific form in which it is presented in II, 7. In the same way many other cross-links connect the three parts of the book which, generally speaking, do not deal with independent branches of a compound system but rather with the various aspects of *one* social, economic, and historical theory.

With Marx and Engels, as indeed with most writers on the field of social, historical, political thought, books have not only a history of their own, but those histories of books—their times and conditions of birth, their addressees, their very titles, and their further adventures in new editions, translations, etc.— form an inseparable part of the history of the theories themselves. It is, therefore, a deplorable fact that hitherto not only the bourgeois critics of the so-called "Marxian contradictions" but even the most faithful adherents of Marx's materialistic science should have quoted his divers theoretical statements without reference to time, addressees, and other historical indices necessary for their materialistic interpretation. This "orthodox" procedure of quoting Marx's (or even Marx's and Engels') statements quite in the abstract, just as the schoolmen quoted the words of Aristotle or the bible, is quite inadequate for a theoretical study of a given social theory from an historical and materialistic standpoint. We have, therefore, even refrained from imitating the example set by modern scientific works in which every item is quoted by its number only and all other information relegated to an annexed bibliography. We have rather put up with that apparent clumsiness which is unavoidably bound up with an immediate supply of all necessary information on the historical circumstances of each quotation. For the same reason we have made only a scanty use of abbreviations and even translated for further clarity the non-English titles of all books quoted in the text and footnotes. The original titles of books so quoted, as well as all other information not immediately required for the full understanding of the current text, and a detailed explanation of all abbreviations are given in the usual manner in the annexed bibliography.

As to terminology, the reader will find some unusual terms, or usual terms applied with a somewhat modified meaning. This was unavoidable in a book that had to deal with Hegelian and Marxian terms which can by no means be translated into conventional English. We have not availed ourselves of all the liberties which were declared necessary in an article contributed by Engels to the November 1885 issue of *The Commonwealth*. We have refrained from linguistic innovations as far as possible and even from coining new English terms corresponding to the many new-coined German terms used by Hegel, Marx, and present-day Marxists. However, we have followed the advice of Engels to risk a heresy rather than to render the difficult German words and phrases by more or less indefinite terms which do not grate upon our ears but obscure the meaning of Marx. Thus, for example, we speak of "production-relations" rather than "relationships," and in dealing with the first and foremost principle of Marx's materialistic method the term of "specification" is used without quotes although we are aware that this term means something more here than it connotes in every-day language. All such terms have been fully explained at their first occurrence and even several times whenever this seemed necessary for a full understanding of the argument.

PART ONE
SOCIETY

CHAPTER I

MARXISM AND SOCIOLOGY

WHAT is the relationship between Marxism and modern sociological teaching? If we think of the Sociology begun by Comte and in fact first named by him, we shall not find any affinity or link between it and Marxism. Marx and Engels, with all their keen desire to extend and enhance the knowledge of society, paid no attention to either the name or contents of that ostensibly new approach to the social studies. Nor were they impressed by the gains the Comtist school made among the progressive intelligentsia of their time. It appears from their correspondence that Marx at one time in the sixties, with his main attention concentrated on the final manuscript of his principal work, picked up from the shelves of the British Museum and read through Comte's *Cours de philosophie positive* of 1830-42, "because the English and French make such a fuss about the fellow."[1] Yet there is even more evidence in the text of *Capital* itself that this reading left no mark in his theoretical work.[2] On still another occasion, in writing to an otherwise highly esteemed Comtist, Marx made it perfectly clear that he was "thoroughly opposed to Comtism as a politician" and had "a very poor opinion of it as a man of science."[3]

Marx's attitude is theoretically and historically well founded.

[1] See Marx's letter to Engels of 7.7.1866 (MEGA, III, iii, p. 345).

[2] See the ironic dismissal of "Comtist recipes for the cookshops of the future" in Marx's reply to the reviewer of *Capital* in the Paris *Revue positiviste*, contained in postscript to second edition of *Capital*, 1872-73, and a casual reference to "Comte and his school" in a footnote to *Capital*, I, p. 297. These are the only instances where Comte's name occurs in *Capital*, while Spencer's name does not occur at all. He is curtly mentioned, along with some other contemporary writers of "pseudo-scientific" economic articles in the *Westminster Review*, in Marx's letter to Engels of 23.5.68 (MEGA, III, iv, p. 58).

[3] See Marx's letter to Beesly of 12.6.71.

The science of socialism as formulated by Marx, owed nothing to this "sociology" of the 19th and 20th centuries which originated with Comte and was propagated by Mill and Spencer. It would be more correct to say that since the days when young Auguste Comte, hitherto the most enthusiastic disciple of the Utopian socialist St. Simon, suddenly broke with his "great master" to work out his own pedantic system of a "positivistic" sociology from a few of the formidable mass of ideas continuously poured forth by that excessively productive mind,[1] bourgeois social thought has been a reaction against the theory and thus also against the practice of modern socialism.[2] Up to the present day "sociologists" have endeavoured to submit another way of answering the embarrassing questions first raised by the rising proletarian movement. From this standpoint only is it possible to understand the essential unity of the manifold theoretical and practical tendencies which during the last hundred years have found their expression under the common denomination of Sociology.

Marxism, then, stands in a much more original and direct relationship to those new problems which modern historic development has put on the agenda of present-day society, than the whole of the so-called "sociology" of Comte, Spencer, and their followers. Bourgeois sociologists refer to the revolutionary socialist science of the proletariat as an "unscientific mixture of theory and politics." Socialists, on the other hand, dismiss the whole bourgeois sociology as mere "ideology."

[1] See Engels' letter to Toennies of 24.1.95, quoted in Gustav Mayer's *Friedrich Engels*, vol. II, p. 552 (first German edition, Berlin, 1933), and, for a non-partisan confirmation of his statement, among others, the faithful report given by Levy-Bruhl in *La philosophie d'Auguste Comte*, 1900, p. 8.

[2] For a brilliant discussion of the historical dispute between Positivism and Marxism, see the concluding paragraphs of Antonio Labriola's reply to Th. G. Masaryk's *Philosophical and Historical Foundations of Marxism*, first published in Rivista Italiana di sociologia, Rome, 1899; here quoted from the second French edition of his *Essais sur la conception matérialiste de l'histoire*, Paris, 1928, p. 311.

There is, however, quite a different relation between the Marxian theory and another body of social thought which descended from an earlier time when the name of "sociology" had not yet been invented, but "society" had already been discovered and recognized along with physical nature as an equally material and important realm of human knowledge and human action.

As Marx himself records in 1859,[1] he embarked upon his new materialistic theory of society, sixteen years before, because of certain grave doubts which had recently assailed his belief in the idealistic philosophy of Hegel. He had at that time just gone through the new and stimulating experiences of his first short period of political activity. As an editor of the *Rheinische Zeitung* (1842-43) he had for the first time found himself called upon to take part in the discussion of "so-called material interests." He had thus been led to occupy himself with "economic questions." On the other hand, he had become aware of the decisive importance which a closer study of the ideas of "French socialism and communism" was bound to have for the furtherance of revolutionary developments in Germany. While the combined effect of all these new impulses had already considerably undermined his faith in the old Hegelian formulæ, the real nature of that Prussian State which had been so sublimely exalted by Hegel was finally revealed to him by a most conclusive personal experience. He was compelled to resign from the staff of the *Rheinische Zeitung* which under his leadership within less than a year had become the most conspicuous organ of the progressive movement in pre-revolutionary Germany. Nor was his withdrawal sufficient, as had been hoped by the frightened managers, to arrest the judgment of suppression pronounced against the *Rheinische Zeitung* by an equally frightened government.

[1] See Marx's Preface to his *Critique of Political Economy*, 1859—hereafter referred to as *"Preface* 1859."

Thus confronted with an increasing number of striking discrepancies between his philosophical creed and his actual experiences, Marx turned once more to Hegel. A detailed "critical revision" of Hegel's *Philosophy of Law*, on which he concentrated for the next five months,[1] led him to the conclusion that

legal relations as well as forms of State cannot be understood out of themselves nor out of the so-called general development of the human mind but, on the contrary, are rooted in the material conditions of life, the aggregate of which Hegel, following the precedent of the English and French of the 18th century, grouped together under the name of "civil society," and that the anatomy of civil society is to be sought for in Political Economy.

We see here the decisive significance which the concept of "civil society" had gained for the young Marx who was then just passing from Hegelian idealism to his later materialistic theory. While still formally basing his criticism of Hegel's glorification of the State on the realistic statements concerning the nature of civil society embodied in the same Hegelian work, Marx now definitely abandoned Hegel and all his idealistic philosophy. Instead, he associated himself with those great enquirers into the social nature of man who, in the preceding centuries, had first set up the new idea of Civil Society as a revolutionary slogan, and had even unearthed, in the new science of Political Economy, the material foundations of that new and "civilized" form of society.[2]

Hegel, indeed, had not derived the deep realistic knowledge which, under the heading of *Civil Society*[3], stands out in such

[1] See the comprehensive *MSS. of 1843*, now published in MEGA, I, 1, i, pp. 401-553.

[2] See, for example, Adam Ferguson, *An Essay on the History of Civil Society*, 1767, and Adam Smith, *An Inquiry into the Nature and Causes of the Wealth of Nations*, 1776.

[3] See Hegel, *Philosophy of Law*, Part III, sec. 2, esp. §§ 188 *et seq.* ("System of Needs"), §§ 230 *et seq.* ("Police").

sharp relief against the rest of his book from an independent study of the as yet extremely backward conditions of German society. He took both the name and contents of his "civil society" ready-made from the French and English social philosophers, politicians, and economists. Behind Hegel, as Marx said, stood the "English and French of the 18th century" with their new discoveries of the structure and movement of society who, in their turn, reflected the real historical development which culminated in the Industrial Revolution in England after the middle of the 18th century and in the great French Revolution of 1789-1815.

Marx, then, in developing his new socialist and proletarian science, took his cue from that early study of society which, although first communicated to him by Hegel, had really been born of the revolutionary epoch of the bourgeoisie. This appears most strikingly in his complete adoption of the scientific results of classical Political Economy as developed by Petty and Bois-guillebert, Quesnay, Smith, and Ricardo, and taken from them by Marx's immediate predecessors, the German idealist philosophers Kant, Fichte, and Hegel. There is, so far, not much difference between Marx's reference to Political Economy as an "anatomy of civil society," and Hegel's philosophical attempt to base the State on Civil Society, and Civil Society on the "System of Needs" as explored by the new science of "Political Economy." He had even more expressly, in an earlier study, described the "system of needs" as the "first form of government," underlying such higher developed forms as the State and the law. Yet there is this tremendous difference from the outset that Hegel had all along used the realistic knowledge borrowed from the classical economists only for the purpose of enhancing the importance of his ultimately idealistic system, while Marx made Political Economy the pivot of a wholly materialistic theory of society.

The very pungency with which Marx in his later writings

repeatedly pointed out that post-classical bourgeois economy (the so-called "vulgar" economy) had not advanced beyond Ricardo in any important points, and scornfully dismissed the new socio-scientific synthesis of Comte's "Positivism" for the infinitely greater achievement of Hegel,[1] shows once more the lasting importance of that early phase of economic and social thought for the theory of Marx. This is true even though he far transcended those older theories in asserting the new development of society and the new needs and aims of the proletariat, now arising as an independent class. The proletariat guided by Marxian theory is therefore not only, as Friedrich Engels put it, "the inheritor of German classical philosophy."[2] It is also the inheritor of classical bourgeois economics and social research. As such, it has transformed the traditional classical theory in accordance with the intervening changes in historical conditions.

Marx no longer regards bourgeois society from the standpoint of its first phase of development and its opposition to the feudal structure of mediæval society. He is not interested only in the static laws of its existence. He treats bourgeois society in all its aspects as a transitory historical phenomenon. He explores the whole process of its genesis, and the tendencies contained therein which, in their further development, will lead to its revolutionary overthrow. He finds these tendencies twofold : *objective* in the economic basis of bourgeois society, *subjective* in the new division of social classes arising out of this same economic basis and not out of politics, law, ethics, etc. Thus "civil society," which until then had constituted a homogeneous whole, opposed only to feudalism, is now torn into two opposed "parties." The assumed "civil society" is in reality "bourgeois society," namely,

[1] See *Capital* I, p.p. 47-48, footnote 32, and *Theories of Surplus Value*, III, pp. 571-76, and the above-mentioned letter to Engels of 7.7.66.
[2] See the concluding sentence of Engels' book on *Ludwig Feuerbach and the End of Classical Philosophy*, 1888, and an additional reference to the equal importance of the "developed economic and political conditions in England and France," in the Preface to the first German edition of his pamphlet on *Socialism, Utopian and Scientific*, 1882.

a society based on the cleavage of classes, in which the bourgeois class controls other classes economically and therefore politically and culturally. So at last "la classe la plus laborieuse et la plus misérable" enters the widened horizon of social science. Marxian theory recognizes the class war of the oppressed and exploited wage labourers to be a war for the abolition of present-day society. As a materialistic science of the contemporary development of bourgeois society, Marxian theory is at the same time a practical guide for the proletariat in its struggle to realize proletarian society.

The later artificial detachment of sociology as a special branch of learning, which dates its scientific origin from Comte, and at its best allows the great original thinkers who did the real productive work in this field to stand as its "forerunners," represents nothing more than an escape from the practical, and therefore also theoretical, tasks of the present historical epoch. Marx's new socialist and proletarian science which, in a changed historical situation, further developed the revolutionary theory of the classical founders of the doctrine of society, is the genuine social science of our time.

CHAPTER II

THE PRINCIPLE OF HISTORICAL SPECIFICATION

MARX comprehends all things social in terms of a definite historical epoch. He criticizes all the categories of the bourgeois theorists of scoiety in which that specific character has been effaced. Already in his first economic work we find him reproaching Ricardo for having applied the specifically bourgeois concept of *rent* to "landed property of all epochs and of all countries. This is the error of all economists who represent bourgeois production conditions as eternal."[1]

The scope of the principle of historical specification is clearly demonstrated in this example. *Landed property* has been widely different in character and has played very different parts in the various historical epochs of society. The different ways in which primitive communal property in land had been broken up directly influenced the varied forms of the later development of society based upon private property.[2] Up to the Middle Ages landed property, i.e., agriculture, constituted the central category dominating all the other categories of production, just as *capital* does in present-day bourgeois society.[3] The different ways in which, in different parts of the world, feudal property in land, upon the victory of the bourgeois mode of production, was subjected to capital, the different ways in which rent was transformed into a part of capitalistic surplus value, and agriculture into an industry, determined to a great extent the structure of

[1] See *Misère de la philosophie*, 1847 (MEGA, I, vi, p. 217).
[2] See *Critique of Political Economy*, 1859, p. 9, footnote 1.
[3] See the MSS. of a *General Introduction* to the *Critique of Political Economy*, dated 25.8.57, first printed in *Neue Zeit*, XXI, i, pp. 710 *et seq.* (1903)—afterwards referred to as *Introduction*, 1857.

the various capitalistic systems which arose therefrom. They retain an importance even for the forms of the labour movements which were later to arise within them, and for the different forms in which the transition to the socialist mode of production will ultimately be effected in each of the different systems. For this reason Marx investigated with particular care, to the end of his life, the history of landed property and rent as shown on the one hand in the *United States*, and on the other hand in *Russia*. Similarly, Lenin, in his book on *The Development of Capitalism in Russia*, at the end of the 19th century, analysed the specific historical forms of this transitionary process.[1] Yet all this comprehensive study of the various historical forms, serves only, both with Marx and Lenin, as a base for the working out of the specific character of *capitalistic rent* in the fully developed *bourgeois society*.

In the fundamental analysis of the modern *Capitalistic Mode of Production* which forms the subject matter of the first book of *Capital*, Marx does not deal with the category of rent at all. What is discussed here, in addition to the general function of the soil as an element of the labour process itself,[2] is only the manner in which the historical transition to the modern capitalistic mode of production reacted upon the conditions of the agricultural proletariat, first, in fully developed industrial countries,[3] second, in such countries as Ireland that have fallen behind in the process of industrialization,[4] and finally in actual colonies.[5] The proper place for a discussion of "rent" is in a section of the third book of *Capital* in which the forms of *Capitalistic Distribution* are

---

[1] Lenin began to write this book in 1896 while he was in prison and went on with it during his exile in Siberia. The first Russian edition appeared in 1899, the second in 1907. German edition in vol. III of *Collected Works*, Vienna-Berlin, 1929.

[2] See *Capital*, I, pp. 139 et seq.

[3] *Ibid*, pp. 639 et seq.

[4] *Ibid*, pp. 664 et seq.

[5] *Ibid*, the whole chapters xxiv and xxv dealing with *So-called Primitive Accumulation* and *Modern Colonial System*.

analysed, as they arise from the historical forms of Capitalistic Production.[1] Even here, there is no room for an independent analysis of earlier historical forms. A few scattered remarks serve to illuminate the contrast between the modern bourgeois form of landed property and past historical forms ; and consideration of the historical *Genesis of Capitalistic Rent* is relegated to a supplementary chapter at the end.[2]

"Rent," then, as discussed in the Marxian theory, is in no way a general term referring to landed property of all epochs. It refers to "a specific historical form into which feudal land ownership and small peasants' agriculture have been *transformed* through the influence of capital and of the capitalistic mode of production."[3] In this sense, and in this sense only, an analysis of modern capitalistic rent, or of the portion of the surplus value produced by the industrial capital which falls into the hands of the capitalistic landowner, forms a necessary part of the complete analysis of the process of capitalistic production contained in the three books of *Capital*.

The principle of historical specification is further demonstrated by the way Marx deals with the different historical forms of "capital" itself. Just as in the present epoch *Industrial Capital* appears as the standard form of all capital, so did *"Merchants' Capital"* and its twin brother, *"Interest-bearing Capital,"* and the various sub-forms of these (more exactly described by Marx as "capital for trading in goods," "capital for trading in money," "capital for lending money"), occupy an independent and, in certain respects, a predominating position in the epochs preceding capitalistic society and, indeed, in the first phases of capitalist society itself. Even within the fully developed capitalist economy of to-day the merchant and the banker, though not involved in actual production like the industrial capitalist, perform a definite

[1] See *Capital*, III, ii, pp. 153-348.
[2] *Ibid*, pp. 315-348.   [3] *Ibid*, pp. 153 *et seq.*

function in the circulation of capital. They also participate in the distribution of the "surplus value ;"a considerable part of the yearly amount at the disposal of the capitalist class as a whole falls to their share as "commercial profit" and "interest"—just as we have seen another part of it going in the form of "rent" to the landed-property-owners who have as little to do with actual production. Moneylenders' capital has even recaptured an important position—though not, as some Marxists have recently believed, a definite supremacy—in its new form as an integral part of the modern so-called "finance capital," i.e., a system of highly concentrated capital obtained by the fusion of private and State-controlled bank capital with trust and State-controlled industrial capital.[1]

The Marxian analysis of modern capitalistic production starts from the assumption that the previously independent forms of trading-capital and money-capital have been *transformed* into mere accessories of the now prevailing form. It is true that all capitalistic production bears the stamp of its historical origin from the intrusion of the merchant into the sphere of feudal production. Capitalistic production remains, even to-day, essentially a *production for sale*. Every article resulting from capitalistic production is to be sold as a commodity, whether to another industrial capitalist who needs it for carrying on his own process of production or, ultimately, to the immediate consumer. Again, all capitalistic production is conditioned by a given amount of disposable *money*. Thus the very way in which "capital" first arose and gained control of production through the money supplied by wealthy individuals, merchants, usurers, etc., constantly repeats itself under the present conditions of a fully developed industrial production. "Every new aggregate of capital," says Marx, "comes on the stage, that is, on the market, whether of commodities, labour, or money, even in our days,

[1] See Hilferding, *Finance Capital*, 1910, and Lenin, *Imperialism as the last stage of Capitalism*, 1917.

in the form of money that by a definite process has to be transformed into capital."[1]

Nevertheless the "secret," not only of "how capital produces" but also of "how capital *is* produced"—and incidentally the key to the abolition of all capitalistic exploitation and wage slavery —can in no way be discovered through an analysis of the functions performed by those "accessory" forms of capital in the process of circulation, or of the revenues which accrue to the capitalists concerned, in consideration of the "services" performed in that sphere. "One will therefore understand," says Marx, "why in our analysis of the basic form of capital, of the form in which it determines the economic organization of modern society, its popular, and, as it were, antediluvian forms, 'trading capital' and 'usurers' capital,' for the present (viz., in the analysis of the actual process of the capitalistic production in the first book of *Capital*) are entirely ignored."[2]

Even when, in the second and third books of *Capital*, Marx comes back to these "antediluvian forms" in dealing with Capitalistic Circulation and Distribution, he takes as his main theme not their historical development but only the specific forms into which they have been *transformed* by the action of modern industrial capital.[3] The historical analyses which run through the whole of the sections concerned, and both of the supplementary chapters under the headings "*Historical data concerning merchants' capital*" and "*Pre-capitalistic conditions,*"[4] merely serve to enlighten that great historical process through which, in the course of centuries and millenaries, *trade* and *money transactions* lost more and more of their originally dominating position until they assumed their present place as mere sub-

[1] See *Capital*, I, p. 109, and, for a more detailed analysis of the various forms which capital assumes in its different stages, II, i.
[2] *Ibid*, p. 126.
[3] *Ibid*, II, i-iv; III, xvi, xix, xxi-xxxv.
[4] *Ibid*, III, xx and xxxvi.

ordinate modes of existence of the various functions which industrial capital sometimes adopts and sometimes discards within the sphere of its circulation.

There is one aspect alone under which *rent* as well as *trading capital* and *money-capital* might have been treated as a proper theme in Marx's analysis of the modern capitalistic mode of production. According to an original and more comprehensive scheme of procedure, Marx would have followed up the more strictly economic topics of production, circulation and distribution, social classes, etc., as now discussed in the three books of *Capital*, by an investigation of what may be called "economic questions of a higher order" such as the relation between *town and country* and the *international relations of production.*[1]

Only with these later researches would Marx's analysis have reached the point where the antagonism of *landed property* to *capital*, as well as that of *trade and money-capital* to *industrial capital*, survives in present-day society :—the latter as a characteristic difference in general structure and outlook between trading cities and factory towns, commercial and industrial States ; the former as a persisting conflict between the aims of the rural farmers and the industrial and commercial interests represented by the towns ; and, on an international scale, between primarily agricultural and definitely industrial countries.

The principle of historical specification as illustrated by the preceding examples (landed property and the various forms of capital) is strictly adhered to by Marx. He deals with all categories of his economic and socio-historical research in that specific form and in that specific connection in which they appear in

[1] See *Introduction*, 1857, pp. 778-79, and *Capital*, I, p. 317, where Marx expressly states that he cannot here go further into the cleavage between town and country, although "the whole economic history of society is summed up in the movement of this antagonism." For a more detailed discussion see the author's introduction to his edition of Marx's *Capital*, Berlin, 1932, pp. 8 *et seq.*

modern bourgeois society.[1] He does not treat them as eternal categories. Nor does he, for that matter, transform himself into an historian. While fully aware of the different specific forms in which many economic categories of modern bourgeois society had occurred in earlier epochs, he does not go into the history of "money," of "exchange of commodities," of "wage-labour," or of that of "co-operation," "division of labour," etc. He discusses the different stages of the historical development of all these economic concepts, and of the political, juridical, and other ideological concepts bound up with them, only in so far as it is necessary for his main theme, i.e. the specific character assumed by them in modern bourgeois society.

The contrast which exists in this respect between Marx and his forerunners comes out most strikingly upon comparison. While the work of the last representative of classical bourgeois economy, David Ricardo, is devoted to the *"Principles of Political Economy,"* Marx restricted his economic research to "modern bourgeois production"[2] and finally gave the work which contains his analysis and critique of the whole of traditional Political Economy the plain and definite name *"Capital."* Ricardo begins the exposition of his system with the general concept of "value" ; Marx commences the critical investigation of the theory and the facts underlying modern bourgeois economy with an external object, a palpable thing, "commodity." While Ricardo frees the economic concept of "value" from the last earthly impurities that were still attached to it by his predecessors, Marx regards even the more concrete term of "commodity" as still too abstract to serve as a starting point for his critical analysis of modern bourgeois production. He therefore excludes from his application of the term those cases in which an exchange of commodities has occurred as an *isolated phenomenon*, under entirely different historical conditions. He deals with

[1] See *Introduction*, 1857, pp. 774 *et seq.*
[2] *Ibid*, p. 712.

30

"commodity" only as an offshoot of the *general commodity production*" prevailing in modern industrial society. The single commodity, then, is not an independent entity. It is but one of the units into which that "immense collection of commodities," which had been defined by the classical economists as the "*wealth of nations*," is to be resolved for the purpose of scientific investigation. It is an element of that mass of exchangeable products which Marx, by a most significant alteration of the accepted Smithian term, called the "*bourgeois wealth*"[1] or, more precisely, the "*wealth of those societies in which the capitalistic mode of production prevails.*"[2] Only thus specifically defined do "commodities" form the subject matter of Marx's economic analysis. Only as properties of a commodity so defined do the general concepts of "*value in use*" and "*value in exchange*," and the other terms of the classical economic system derived from those fundamental concepts, interest him.

This applies even to the most general term of "*value*" which, according to Marx, must still be distinguished from "value in exchange"—the latter being only the external form in which the intrinsic "value" of a given commodity manifests itself in the ratio of exchange of such commodities.[3] This most abstract term, which Marx adopted from the later classical economists, has been highly suspect to some well-meaning but superficial interpreters of Marx who found that the concept of an intrinsic "value," distinct from exchange-value, recks of scholasticism, metaphysical realism, Hegelian idealism, and what not, and for this reason does no credit to a "materialistic" science. As a matter of fact, the somewhat "minute" Marxian analysis of the "form of value or value in exchange" as contained in a section of the first chapter of *Capital*, has not unjustly been indicted, as Marx himself anticipated it to be,[4] on the count of difficulty. Never-

---

[1] See *Critique of Political Economy*, 1859, opening sentence.
[2] See *Capital*, I, 1867, opening sentence.   [3] *Ibid*, pp. 2-5.
[4] See *Preface* to first edition of *Capital*, 1867.

theless, there is no point in accepting the term "exchange value," as taken by Marx from his forerunners, the founders of classical Political Economy, and rejecting that of an intrinsic "value" which was used by him only as a means to work out more clearly the true contents of the classical value concept, and to expose critically the "Fetishism" bound up with the term as used by his predecessors.[1]

The Marxian interpretation of "value" is far removed from that peculiar misconception by which some earlier writers had held it to be a physical property belonging to things along with those other physical properties which establish the utility of such things for human wants or their "use-value." Nor did he share the more refined mistake which at his time, in spite of several refutations, still lingered in the minds of the economists, and by which "value" was regarded as a metaphysical property belonging, not to the things themselves nor to their substance but, as it were, to "things in exchange." Value, according to Marx, is first of all no physical property. "So far no chemist has ever discovered exchange-value either in a pearl or in a diamond."[2] The value pertaining to useful things when they are exchanged as commodities may well be called a "meta-physical" quality, but only in that extremely unmetaphysical sense of being *not a physical but a social quality*, applying to the products of human labour or rather to the labour itself by which such useful things

---

[1] It is interesting to note in this connection that Marx introduced the term of "value," as distinct from "value in exchange," into the statement of his theory as late as 1867, while he had not used it in an otherwise identical exposition of his argument in 1859. He did so, in the writer's opinion, mainly for the sake of clarifying the more detailed critical exposure of the *Fetishism of Commodities* which was now added, in the first chapter of *Capital*, to the earlier statement of the theory, as contained in the *Critique of Political Economy*. In fact, as will be shown in Part II of this book, the mere theoretical contents of the Marxian argument can be expressed just as accurately, though perhaps not quite as definitely, without using the term of "value" at all. But it is different with the more important critical implications of the term.

[2] See *Capital*, I, pp. 49-50.

are produced and to the labourers producing them within a "commodity-producing society," i.e., under the conditions prevailing in present-day capitalistic society.

Modern economists have tried to improve upon classical economic theory by pointing to the fact that "value" is not a property pertaining to a thing (or to the members of a class of things), but is rather a *relation* connecting two or more things, and Jevons has made much of that "discovery." In fact, there is nothing particularly new in this Jevonsian "relativism" as against those classical writers who had defined the value pertaining to "things of exchange" as a purely quantitative relation, and it altogether misses the point where the classical concept of "value" was indeed vulnerable. Marx was fully conscious of the fact that all concepts of "value" are strictly "relative" terms. They either denote an immediate relation between objects and man (which is realized by actual "use" or consumption), or a relation of a different order (realized by the "exchange" of such objects), viz., the quantitative relation in which use-values of one sort are exchanged for those of another sort whenever they are exchanged. The relations of the latter order had been regarded by the classical economists as the only "value" to be dealt with in a strictly economic science, and had been styled by them "value in exchange," as distinguished from mere utility or "value in use." Marx easily agreed with the classical writers when they established the difference in kind prevailing between *"exchange-value"* as a quantitative relation arising through the selling and buying of commodities on the market, i.e., by a social process ; and *"use-value"* as a merely qualitative relation between external objects and man. But he did not agree with them in the *ultimate location* of the social relations manifesting themselves in the "value" relations of commodities as established by their exchange. For the purpose of bringing out the point which really interested him, he made use of the as yet vague distinction, made by the classicists, between "exchange-

33

value" as the apparent phenomenon and "value" as the hidden entity underlying its appearance. By an apparently notional development (in the best Hegelian style) of the various connotations of the classical term of "value," he in fact disclosed the real social nature of the *fundamental human relations* underlying the so-called "value" of the classicists. They do not arise between the commodities as exchanged on the market nor, for that matter, between the persons selling and buying such commodities, but rather they are previously established by the definite forms in which the workers producing such commodities co-operate in their production under the control of the capitalist. Thus, the relation manifested by the "value" of things is essentially a *"social relation of production" arising between men and men.* Indeed, as we shall see in a more detailed way in the second part of this book, the main result of Marx's "Critique" of the traditional theory of Political Economy consists in the discovery and description of these fundamental social relations of men—relations which, for a definite historical epoch, appear to the subjects concerned in the disguised and, as it were, perverted form of relations of things, viz., as "value-relations" of the commodities co-operatively produced by them and mutually exchanged on the market.

"Value" then, in all its denominations, like other economic things or relations such as "commodity," "money," "labour-power," "capital," etc., means to Marx a *socio-historical fact* or something which though not described in physical terms is still empirically given in a strictly verifiable manner.[1] "We must always keep in mind in dealing with economic theory, as indeed with all other socio-historical science, that the subject matter, here modern bourgeois society, is given in the mind of the observer just as it is in reality, and that its categories express,

---

[1] See Marx's letter to Engels 2.4.58, in which he says that this concept of value "although an abstraction, is an *historical abstraction* which, therefore, could only be made on the basis of a determinate economic development of society." (MEGA, III. ii, p. 309.)

therefore, forms of being, modes of existence, and often only single aspects of this definite society or subject matter."[1]

We shall later study the far-reaching theoretical and practical implications of the difference between this Marxian principle of historical specification and the abstract concepts of classical Political Economy. We here confine ourselves to one most important result. The concept of "*commodity*" in the specific form and context in which it appears under the conditions of the present system of "capitalistic commodity production," includes from the very beginning a commodity of a peculiar nature, incorporating the flesh and blood in the hands and heads of the wage-labourers—the commodity *labour-power*. "These labourers who have to sell themselves piecemeal are a commodity like every other article of commerce, and are consequently exposed to all the vicissitudes of competition, to all the fluctuations of the market."[2] Furthermore, the sellers of that peculiar commodity, under the very condition of its sale, are never in the position of free agents,[3] for they "live only so long as they find work, and find work only so long as their labour increases capital."[4]

Thus the term of "commodity" as used by Marx presupposes the transformation of labour power into a commodity, and "commodity production" is equivalent to present-day *capitalistic commodity production*.[5] Only by bearing this in mind can we understand the importance of that general analysis of "Commodity" which in Marx's book precedes all further analysis and critique of the economic conditions prevailing in present society.

[1] See *Introduction*, 1857, p. 777. See also the preceding remark on p. 774 where Marx, opposing his own "theoretical" method to that hitherto applied by the classical theorists, emphasized the same point : "Even when applying a theoretical method we must bear in mind the subject, society, as our real pre-supposition."
[2] See *Communist Manifesto*, 1848 (MEGA, I, vi, p. 532).
[3] See the Report of the Inspectors of Factories of the six months ending April 30th, 1850 ; p. 45—quoted by Marx in *Capital*, I, p. 310.
[4] See *Communist Manifesto*, 1848 (MEGA, I, vi, p. 532).
[5] See *Capital*, I, p. 133, footnote 41 ; see also II, pp. 9, 11 *et seq.*, 88, etc.

It is only thus that the distinctive historical conditions of the present epoch of a fully developed capitalistic mode of production can be brought out in full relief without cutting them off from their more general, but equally historical, background. *Commodity*, according to Marx, *means capital ;* but capital, both historically and theoretically, means a lot more than a mere exchange of commodities. Marx is aware of the "definite historical conditions" which are necessary that a product may become a "commodity" and that, in the further development, "money" may appear as the general commodity, for the purpose of exchange. "The appearance of products as *commodities* presupposed such a development of the social division of labour, that the separation of use-value from exchange-value, a separation which first began with barter, must already have been completed." Again, "the particular functions of *money* which it performs, either as the mere equivalent of commodities, or as means of circulation, or means of payment, as hoard, or as universal money, point to very different stages in the process of social production."[1] Yet we know by experience that a relatively primitive development of society suffices for the production of all these forms. *It is otherwise with capital.* "The historical conditions of its existence are by no means given with the mere circulation of money and commodities. It can spring into life only when the owner of the means of production and subsistence meets in the market with the free labourer selling his labour-power. And this one historical condition comprises a world's history. Capital, therefore, announces from its first appearance a new epoch in the process of social production."[2]

Only at this stage are we able to grasp the full importance of *industrial capital* as the only form which adequately represents the nature of modern capitalistic production. "Industrial capital," according to an express assertion of Marx which we may safely take to be his final and most complete statement on

[1] See *Capital*, I, pp. 32.   [2] *Ibid.*; see also II, p. 13.

this matter, "gives to production its capitalistic character. Its existence includes that of class antagonism between capitalists and labourers. To the extent that it assumes control over social production, the technique and social organization of the labour process are revolutionized and with them the economic and historical type of society. The other kinds of capital, which appear before the industrial capital amid past or declining conditions of social production, are not only subordinated to it and suffer changes in the mechanism of their functions corresponding with it, but move on it as a basis ; they live and die, stand and fall, as this, their basis, lives and dies, stands and falls."[1]

[1] See *Capital*, II, p. 29.

CHAPTER III

THE PRINCIPLE OF HISTORICAL SPECIFICATION (continued)

THE principle of historical specification, besides its theoretical significance as an improved method of sociological analysis and research, becomes of first-rate importance as a polemical weapon in the practical struggle waged against the existing conditions of society. The manner in which this weapon is wielded by the Marxists appears most clearly in a section of the *Communist Manifesto* of 1848, dealing with "the bourgeois objections to communism."[1] One basic form of argument recurs in all the replies to the bourgeois indictment of communism. In answer to the accusation that they want to abolish property, individuality, liberty, culture, law, family, "fatherland," etc., the communists say that the point at issue is not the general conditions of all social life but only the specific historical form assumed by them in present-day bourgeois society, All economic, class, and other characters constituting that specific historical form are discussed, with the result that the would-be defenders of the natural and necessary foundations of society are revealed to be the biassed protagonists of the particular conditions of the existing bourgeois order and the particular needs of the bourgeois class.

The first objection raised by the bourgeoisie is that the Communists want to abolish *property*. To this, the Manifesto replies :

The abolition of existing property relations is not a peculiar feature of Communism. All property relations in the past have been continually subject to historical change.

The French revolution, for example, abolished feudal property in favour of bourgeois property.

[1] See MEGA, I, vi, pp. 538-44 ; also p. 528.

38

The distinguishing feature of Communism is not the abolition of all property, but the abolition of bourgeois property.

But modern bourgeois private property is the final and most complete expression of the system of producing and appropriating products that is based on class antagonisms, on the exploitation of the many by the few.

In this sense, the theory of the Communists may be summed up in the single sentence : abolition of private property.

It is then further argued that this modern form of property can no longer be described as a "hard-won, personally acquired property" forming "the groundwork of all personal freedom, activity and independence." A property answering that ideological concept of the theoretical spokesmen of the bourgeoisie was "the property of the petty artisan and of the small peasant," a form of property that existed before the bourgeois form. The communists have no need to abolish that. "The development of industry has abolished it and is abolishing it daily." "The present form of property moves in the antagonism of capital and wage-labour." It has a specific and different significance for each of the two great classes confronting each other in modern bourgeois society. "*To be a capitalist is to have not only a personal, but a social, status in production.*" In the same way, wage-labour, the labour of the proletarian, does not create property for the labourer, it creates capital, i.e., the social power that exploits wage-labour. "The abolition of property, therefore, does not mean the transformation of personal property into social property ; it is only the social character of the property that undergoes a change, it loses its class character."

The second objection of the bourgeoisie is that the communists want to destroy *individuality* and *freedom*. Communism replies that what is at stake here is only the "bourgeois individuality, independence and freedom :"

39

By freedom is meant, under the present bourgeois conditions of production : free trade, free selling and free buying. But if haggling disappears, free haggling disappears also. This talk about free haggling, and all other braggadoccio of our bourgeoisie about freedom in general, has a meaning, if any, only in contrast with restricted haggling, with the fettered traders of the Middle Ages, but has no meaning when opposed to the Communist abolition of haggling, of the bourgeois conditions of production, and of the bourgeoisie itself.

The bourgeois calls it an "abolition of property" when private property is abolished. But this property exists in the hands of his class only by being cut off from the vast majority of society. From the moment when labour can no more be transformed into capital, money, rent, in one word, into a social power, capable of being monopolized, he complains that "individuality is being destroyed." He confesses, therefore, that by "individuality" he means none other than that of the bourgeois, i.e., the capitalistic owner of property. "This individuality must, indeed, be destroyed."

In the same way, the bourgeoisie confuses the general concept of *work*, and *activity*, with the specific bourgeois form of wage-labour, the forced labour of the property-less labourer for the benefit of the non-labouring owners of capital. If the bourgeoisie is afraid lest "with the abolition of private property all activity will cease and universal laziness overtake us," the Manifesto rejoins :

According to this, bourgeois society ought long ago to have been wrecked through sheer idleness ; for those of its members who work acquire nothing, and those who acquire anything do not work. The whole of this objection is but another expression of the tautology : There can no longer be any wage-labour where there is no longer any capital.

Next, the bourgeoisie laments the threatened loss of *culture* through the advent of Communism. To this complaint also, Marx has a specific reply :

Just as to the bourgeois the disappearance of class property is the disappearance of production itself, so the disappearance of class culture is to him identical with the disappearance of all culture.

That culture the loss of which he laments is, for the enormous majority, a mere training to act as a machine.

The same lack of discernment as in the case of individuality, freedom, and culture, is shown in the sweeping indictment brought against communism on account of its professed hostility to the *State* and the *law*. The so-called "subversive tendencies" of the communists are, in fact, not directed against those general functions of unifying the elements of society into a living and developing whole, which, in the past, have been fulfilled, though in an increasingly defective manner, by State compulsion and coercive law. The real target of the communistic attack is *the present State* which has dropped those historical functions one after another until it has become a mere "executive committee managing the common affairs of the bourgeois class as a whole" —and *the present law* which, by a similar process, has become nothing but "the will of the bourgeoisie made into a law for all —a will whose contents are determined by the material conditions of existence of the bourgeois class."

Abolition of the family ! "Even the most radical," says the *Communist Manifesto*, "flare up at this infamous purpose of the Communists." Once more the Marxist replies specifically ·

On what foundation is the present family, the bourgeois family, based ? On capital, on private gain. In its completely developed form it exists only for the bourgeoisie. But it finds its complement in the forcible absence of the family among the proletarians and in public prostitution.

The communists admit that they want to "abolish the exploitation of children by their parents."

They retort to that ever-recurring, stupid assumption of the professional red-baiter that "Communists want to introduce a

KARL MARX

community of wives," that, on the contrary, "the present system
of bourgeois marriage is in reality a system of wives in common."[1] Besides, it is obvious that "the abolition of the present
system of production must involve the abolition of the community of women arising out of that system, that is, of prostitution both official and unofficial."

To the further charge made by nationalists that communism
is going to "abolish the Fatherland," the Manifesto replies that,
in present-day bourgeois society, "the workers have no Fatherland." "One cannot take from them what they do not have."[2]

The attitude of the proletariat of each country regarding so-
called "national interests" depends on the specific stage reached
by the workers' movement in its historical development on a
national and an international scale :

To the extent that exploitation of one individual by another
is abolished the exploitation of one nation by another is also
abolished.

With the disappearance of the antagonism between classes
within the nation, the hostility of one nation to another will
disappear.

[1] This statement recalls to mind Hume's report (in Essays, XIX) of the
remark a Turkish ambassador made to Voltaire that "you Christians keep
your seraglios without any further expense in the houses of your friends."
See also a similar statement made by the De Goncourts as to the system of
marriage prevailing among the bourgeoisie at their time.

[2] The conclusion that the general idea of "Fatherland" loses all meaning
for the vast majority of the people because "without property, they have
no Fatherland, without Fatherland, everybody is against them, and
themselves must be up in arms against everybody," had already been
brought forward by Brissot in his Observations d'un répuplicain sur les différents
systèmes d'administration provinciales, 1787 (See Marx's excerpts in MEGA,
I, vi, pp. 616-17). Thus it was a bourgeois revolutionist who first enunciated
that most "odious" of all the socialist doctrines which later was expressed
in the "incendiary" statement of the Communist Manifesto : "The workers
have no Fatherland." Yet it was just the bourgeois revolution represented
by Brissot that finally destroyed the last historical remnants of what had
been, according to a later statement of Engels, "for all free men, a real
Fatherland, i.e., an inherited free communal property in land" (See
Engels' article on The Mark, first published as an Appendix to the first
German edition of Socialism, Utopian and Scientific, 1883).

42

In reply to "the indictment levelled against Communism from a religious, philosophical and from an ideological standpoint generally," the Manifesto summarily points to the specific historical character of all human ideas :

What else does the history of ideas prove than that intellectual production changes its character as material production is changed ? The ruling ideas of an age have ever been only the ideas of the ruling class.

When the ancient world was in decline, the ancient religions were conquered by Christianity. When Christian ideas succumbed in the 18th century to the ideas of enlightenment, feudal society fought its death battle with the then revolutionary bourgeoisie. The ideas of religious liberty and freedom of conscience merely expressed the sway of free competition within the domain of knowledge.

This argument holds good also against that more enlightened fraction of the bourgeoisie who concede that religious, moral, philosophical, political, legal ideas, etc., have been modified in the course of historical development but, at the same time, reproach Communism for abolishing the *eternal truths* common to all historical epochs, such as freedom, justice, etc. ; or for *abolishing religion and morality altogether, instead of remoulding them on a new basis.* Marx replies that, even in this most absolute form, the so-called "general ideas" must always have a specific historical element. While they do not depend on the definite form which class oppositions have assumed in any particular epoch of social development, they do depend on the historical fact, continuing through all those epochs, of the existence of class antagonism :

Whatever form they may have taken, one fact is common to all past ages, viz., the exploitation of one part of society by the other. No wonder, then, that the social consciousness of all past ages, despite the multiplicity and variety it displays, moves within certain common forms, or general ideas, which cannot

43

completely vanish, except with the total disappearance of class antagonism.

The communistic revolution is the most radical rupture with traditional property relations.   No wonder, then, that its development involves the most radical rupture with traditional ideas.

CHAPTER IV

THE PRINCIPLE OF CHANGE

TRADITIONAL theory of society, spread over several hundred years and split into many schools and currents, does not present itself to the present-day observer as a homogeneous entity. This is true even if we disregard the fundamental divergence which has occurred within bourgeois thought since the beginning of the 19th century, when a new and predominantly *historical* current opposed itself—at first with a monopolistic claim, later only as a supplementary second form—to the hitherto prevailing *theoretical* approach.

The classical phase of bourgeois social theory, continuing into the first decades of the 19th century, is characterized by an unconscious generalization of the new bourgeois principles. Later, in the hands of the "vulgar" economists of the 19th century, that unsophisticated attitude became a more or less conscious tendency to represent the *economic* system of bourgeois society in contrast to its politics—or at least its basic part, i.e., *production* as distinguished from distribution—as a general and unchangeable form of all social life. Finally, the founders of modern "Economics," and the corresponding schools of "general" or "formal" Sociology, have even raised the "unspecific" treatment of their subject matter to the very principle and criterion of their new and assumedly "disinterested" scientism. A more detailed analysis will be necessary to point out the special manner in which the *a priori* of definite premises evolving out of the historical and class-conditioned position of all bourgeois science, penetrates into the methods and results of each school and into the concepts and propositions set up by the single investigator.

A further complication is added by the fact that, in dealing with contemporary bourgeois social theory, we can often no longer exactly determine how far it represents a reaction to the attack of the proletarian class. Not a few among the most important of its later developments can be directly traced to the Marxian theory. We mention particularly, from the last two generations of German sociologists, jurists, historians, and philosophers, *Toennies* and *Stammler, Max Weber* and *Troeltsch, Scheler* and *Mannheim ;* and among the economists, as not the most important but, perhaps, the most typical representative of this whole group—*Werner Sombart.* The manifold broken and distorted forms assumed by the controversy with Marxism under the particular conditions of German academic science, appear most strikingly in the last-named savant, whose many and extensive writings on modern capitalism and socialism testify by their contents, even more clearly than by the apparent acknowledgment of the author, to the fact that "all that is good in this work is due to the spirit of Marx."[1]

Werner Sombart began his career in the early 90's as what he himself recently, at a conference of the Sociological Society in Zurich, called a "convinced Marxist ;" but later, with the changing political and social conditions leading up to the present régime of a so-called "National Socialism" in Germany, he changed heart and from a disguised Marxist became an altogether undisguised and outright anti-Marxist.[2] Notwithstanding all these subsequent disfigurations, the irresistible influence origin-

[1] See Sombart, *Modern Capitalism,* vol. III (1927), p. xix.

[2] We mention from the writings of Sombart in which this development is reflected, the following: 1894 *et seq.* Review articles and books, Marxist in tendency; among them the first scientific appreciation of the third volume of *Capital* in *Archiv für soziale Bewegung* VII. 1897 First edition of the book *Socialism and Social Movement in the* 19*th Century.* 1900 Pamphlet *Nevertheless ! Theoretical and Historical Notes on the Labour Trade Union Movement.* 1924 Tenth and "entirely revised" edition of the book *Socialism and Social movement* under the changed title *Proletarian Socialism (Marxism).* Subsequent to Hitler's accession to power a new book on *German Socialism,* etc. Refer also to the article on Sombart's future career by Rosa Luxemburg in *Neue Zeit,* XVIII, ii (1899/1900), pp. 740 *et seq.,* and an article by the author in *Archiv für die Geschichte des Sozialismus and der Arbeiterbewegung* XVI.

ally exercised by Marx's theory on all present-day bourgeois social science is clearly evident even in the later career of Sombart. As late as 1928, at the afore-mentioned Conference of the Sociologists, he claimed to have been the first to enunciate the principle of the so-called "non-evaluative character of a genuine sociological science" and, incidentally, traced back that well-known doctrine of contemporary social research to the "contradiction" which forty years before had arisen within himself, that is, between his internal "conviction," and his worldly position as a "Royal Prussian University Professor."[1]

For all these reasons, in confronting the general principles of the Marxian theory with bourgeois science we shall not so much refer to the more recent displays of contemporary social thought in which their persisting difference has already been modified to a certain extent by mutual interaction. We shall rather try to bring out the contrast in the pure form in which it originally appeared in the classical and post-classical bourgeois writers of the 18th and early 19th centuries on the one hand, and in the writings of Marx and Engels on the other.

Classical bourgeois economists concern themselves with existing bourgeois society. They ingenuously regard society's basic relationships as having the immutable character of a genuine natural law, and are for just this reason unable to become aware of any other than this actually given form of society.

Even when bourgeois social theorists appear to speak of other social forms, their real subject matter is the particular form of bourgeois society whose main characteristics they find duplicated in all other forms. When they speak of "society" in general, we can still, with only slight variations, recognize in that so-called general society the well-known features of present-day bourgeois society. This is most evident in the writings of the

[1] See Record of the Proceedings of the Conference of the "Sociological Society," held in Zurich in 1928.

47

great founders of bourgeois social science in the 17th and 18th centuries and their followers, the German idealistic philosophers from Kant to Hegel, who naively used not only the term "society," but even the term "civil society" as a timeless concept.[1]

Even when bourgeois investigators speak of an historical "development" of society, they do not step beyond the magic circle of bourgeois society. They consider all the earlier forms as "preliminary stages" leading up to its present fully developed form. They constantly apply to the preceding historical epochs the concepts drawn from the social conditions existing to-day. Right into the 19th century they described those phases of primitive history which can by no means be represented by the categories of modern bourgeois society, such as, property, State, family, etc., as not belonging to history proper, but merely "prehistoric." Even Johann Gotfried Herder, who stood in a much closer relation to real history than most of his contemporaries, wrote in his "Diary :" "How many ages may have passed by before we learned to know or think ? The Phœnician ? The Ethiopian ? Or none of these ? Are we then, with our Moses, in the right place ?"[2]

Just as in their study of past conditions, so in their conception of the future, bourgeois social theorists remain tied to the bourgeois categories. They simply cannot conceive of any changes other than those set forth in due sequence by a further unfolding of the fundamental principles appearing in present-day bourgeois society. They regard all social revolutions as pathological interferences with "normal" social development.[3] They

[1] See Marx, *The German Ideology* (MEGA, I, v, pp. 25-26).
[2] See J. G. Herder, *Journal meiner Reise*, 1769.
[3] Thus Comte regarded revolutionary periods of society as an analogy to disease in the human body. He did not, for this reason, ignore them totally but rather, following the physician Broussais (who first subjected the phenomena of disease to the laws governing healthy bodies), proclaimed the study of that "pathologie sociale" as a possible substitute for the experimental method used by the physicists.

48

expect, after the revolutionary "cycle" has run its full course, pre-revolutionary *social conditions* to be re-established as unchanged, as, according to a similar theory held by the politicians, the *political conditions* of the ancient régime are re-established in due course by the "Restoration." They hold all tendencies of revolutionary socialism and communism which aim at anything beyond, as mere "disturbances of healthy social progress" and theoretically "unscientific" fantasies.

Marx's social science is opposed to all those traditional concepts of classical bourgeois theory. The contrast is, however, not so simple that it can be reduced to the biblical formula "Let your speech be yea, yea—nay, nay." It would be altogether wrong, for instance, to imagine that since the bourgeois theory is the doctrine of a "bourgeois society," Marx's socialist theory must of necessity be the doctrine of a "socialist society." As a matter of fact, scientific socialism is not at all concerned with the painting of a future state of society. Marx leaves that to the sectarians of the old and new Utopias. According to his materialistic principle, he deals with the real form of society which exists to-day, i.e., bourgeois society. As against the bourgeois "theorists" who continually tend to generalize in one way or another the facts they "discover," he more nearly approaches the method of the bourgeois "historians," from which, however, he keeps himself all the more aloof in another direction through his insistence on a strictly theoretical form of scientific knowledge.

Nor is the bourgeois concept of developmental stages wholly repudiated by Marx. He distinguishes the historical forms of "Asiatic," "Antique" and "Feudal Society," and groups them, together with modern "Bourgeois Society," into a series of *progressive epochs of socio-economic formation.*" Although he no longer regards, as the bourgeois theorists had done, all previous forms of society as mere preliminary steps to its present and fin.

49

formation, still he indulges in the statement that bourgeois society is the last "antagonistic" form of society and as such "concludes the pre-history of a really human society."[1] While he objects to an arbitrary extension of concepts derived from the present bourgeois state of society, he sets forth the principle that bourgeois society, as the "most developed and most complex historical organization of production," furnishes a key to the understanding of earlier epochs of social and economic formation.[2] He even endorsed, in his early years, the "correct idea" underlying that "common fiction of the 18th century which regarded the primitive state of man as the true state of human nature."[3] As we shall see in our further investigation, Marx and Engels adopted a similar attitude in their dealing with the fresh impetus which that Rousseauan slogan of the 18th century had in the meantime received through the discovery of a so-called "primitive communism." From their socialistic point of view, they welcomed the assumption, supported by the leading investigators of the time, of a classless, communistic form preceding all hitherto known society. They did not, however, blindly accept the speculative implications of the new theory, but rather used the historical facts brought forth by Morgan and other explorers of ancient society as a further critical challenge to the "eternal truths" of the more fundamental aspects of the existing class-dominated society.

There is, of course, a much greater difference between the Marxian and the traditional bourgeois approach to the future developments arising from the present state of society. While even the most progressive bourgeois thinkers of the 19th century set their hopes on the slow and gradual process of a so-called

[1] See Preface 1859.
[2] See Introduction, 1857; p. 776.
[3] See The Philosophical Manifesto of the Historical School of Law in Rheinische Zeitung, 1842, No. 221, Supplement (MEGA, I, i, i, p. 251): "The correct idea underlying all these eccentricities (of the Historical School) is that those primitive conditions are naive 'Dutch pictures' of the true conditions."

"evolution," Marx insisted on the inevitability, in a society based on class struggle, of a *social revolution*. Yet in a broader sense the evolutionary concept is not completely wiped out in the Marxian theory. Even the most violent and disruptive revolution remains, according to Marx, a mere step within an historical process through which the productive forces of man, and thus also the whole economic, political, and ideologic structure of society, "evolve" in a solemn and gigantic rhythm from revolution to revolution. Just as there is—in spite of all the intervening revolutions, and, in fact, realized by those revolutions—one progressive line of development leading up from the historic and "prehistoric" past to the contemporary form of bourgeois society, so will the socialist and communist society springing from the revolutionary action of the pro- letarian class, in spite of its break with the established bourgeois order, still remain a further outgrowth of the whole past and present history of an identical "subject" (mankind) acting upon and adapting itself to an identical "object" (nature).[1]

Apart from the revolutionary contents of the Marxian con- cept of development, there is another fundamental difference between the materialistic theory of the historical process and that metaphysical concept of "evolution" which was later, chiefly under the influence of Spencer, blindly accepted by such orthodox Marxists as Kautsky[2] and as blindly rejected by such heterodox Marxists as Georges Sorel, as a principle of scientific sociology.[3] Marx recognized from the outset the delusive character of that so-called "historical evolution," according to which "the last stage regards the preceding stages as only pre- liminary to itself and, therefore, can only look at them one- sidedly.[4] While "orthodox evolutionists" imagined, with

[1] See *Introduction*, 1857; pp. 710 *et seq.*
[2] See the author's *The Materialistic Conception of History (A Critical Examina- tion of the Work of Karl Kautsky)*, Leipzig, 1929, pp. 32 *et seq.*
[3] See Georges Sorel, *Avant-propos* to *Introduction à l'économie moderne*, 1903; also *Illusions du progrés*, third edition, pp. 239-44.
[4] See *Introduction*, 1857, pp. 776-77.

Spencer, that they could explain the more complex organization of the higher types both of animal species and social forms by reference to the simpler organization of the lower, Marx shattered that illusion by the paradoxical statement that *"the anatomy of man is a key to the anatomy of the ape."*[1]

This critical consciousness breaks the magic spell of the metaphysical "law" of evolution. From an *a priori* valid axiom, it is reduced to a working hypothesis which must be empirically verified in each case. Even though bourgeois society does provide a "key" to earlier epochs, it does not follow that such categories as commodity, money, State, law, etc., must have the same meaning for ancient society and its mode of production as they have for modern capitalist production and for the bourgeois society which is based upon it. Thus, the path is made free for a strictly empirical research. Bourgeois society may contain the conditions of earlier societies in a further developed form. It may contain them as well in degenerate, stunted, and travestied forms. Thus the communal property of primitive times, according to Marx, was revived in a travestied form in the Russian "Mir."[2] The present system of society likewise contains within itself the germs of its future developments, though by no means their complete determination. The false idealistic concept of evolution as applied by bourgeois social theorists, is *closed* on both sides, and in all past and future forms of society rediscovers only itself. The new, critical and materialistic Marxian principle of development is, on the contrary, *open* on both sides. Marx does not deal with Asiatic, Antique, or Feudal Society, and still less with those primitive societies which preceded all written history, merely as "preliminary stages" of contemporary society. He regards them, in their totality, as so many independent historical formations which are to be understood within their own categories. In the same way he defines the socialist and communist societies arising out of the prole-

[1] See *Introduction*, 1857, p. 776.　　[2] *Ibid.*

tarian revolution not only as further developed forms of bourgeois society, but as a new type which is no longer to be basically
explained under any of the bourgeois categories. Marx's quarrel
with the *Utopian socialists* is not, as many have imagined, inspired
by their idea of a future commonwealth totally different from
the present state of contemporary bourgeois society. On the
contrary, the weakness of the Utopian socialists lies in the fact
that, in attempting to portray a socialist future, they at bottom
only idealized the existing conditions of society, leaving out the
shadows. All such Utopian schemes will, when worked out in
detail and put into practice, inevitably reproduce only the same
old bourgeois form of society we know so well.[1] On the other
hand, Marxism, while carefully avoiding a detailed painting of
future stages, nevertheless endeavours to find, within contemporary bourgeois society, the main tendencies of a further
development leading up, first to that transitional stage opened
by the proletarian revolution, and ultimately, to those further
advanced stages which Marx called a *completely developed communistic society*. Communistic society in its "first phase," just
emerging from the womb of bourgeois society after protracted
labour pains, will still be determined in many ways in its
economic, political, legal, intellectual, and moral structure by
bourgeois principles. Communistic society in its "second phase,"
where it has already developed on its own basis, will be as far
removed from the principles of present-day bourgeois society
as is, in the other direction, the classless and Stateless "primitive
communism" of the earliest epochs of human society. Communistic society, when it is fully developed, will have left the
narrow bourgeois horizon far behind and will ultimately realize
the principle which, in an abstract manner, was first enunciated
by the "Utopian" pioneers on the threshold of the 19th century :

---

[1] See the third of the articles contributed by Marx to *Neue Rheinische
Zeitung, Politisch-oekonomische Revue*, Hamburg, 1850.

"From each according to his abilities ; to each according to his needs."[1]

To the philosophical dialectic of Hegel, which he otherwise regarded as the perfected instrument of a developmental investigation of society, Marx raised the objection that, although fraught with deep insight into the historical past, it did not genuinely accept the reality of historical change. Hegel, who glorified existing institutions and moderate progress within the narrow confines of the contemporary Prussian state,[2] carefully restricted the validity of his dialectical principle to the *past* developments of society and consigned future progress in a purposely irrational manner to the "mole burrowing below the surface."[3] Even in criticizing the so-called "Pre-formation Hypothesis," according to which all future forms are already physically contained in those that precede them, he emphasized at the same time the correctness of its main idea that social development "remains with itself in its process and that by such a development no new content is brought about, but only a change of form." Developmemt is, therefore, according to Hegel, "only to be regarded as if it were a play ; the something else which is set by it, is in fact nothing else."[4] It is evident that from this standpoint which, in its unyielding Hegelian formula, amounts almost to an involuntary criticism of the principle of evolution as used by the bourgeois social investigators, there is no room for the conscious human-social act, which shall radically transform and overthrow the present order of society. Hegel said, concerning the real "purpose" of all historical action, that "it is already fulfilled in truth, and need not wait for us." Its actual performance, then, serves only "to remove the sem-

[1] See Marx, *Marginal Notes to the Program of the German Labour Party*, 1875 (*Neue Zeit*, IX, i, p. 567).
[2] See Hegel's *Address to his Audience* on the occasion of his *Opening Lecture in Berlin*, Oct. 22nd, 1818.
[3] See the *Peroration* of Hegel's lectures on the *History of Philosophy* (1817-1830).
[4] See Hegel, *Encyclopædia*, I, § 161 (1818-1827).

blance as if it were not yet performed."[1] Hence, in contrast to
some of his followers, who later on actually tried to use his
dialectical method as an instrument for revolution, Hegel
considered the only purpose of his philosophy to be to "re-
establish" the conviction from which "every unsophisticated
consciousness starts :" "*What is rational is real, and what is
real is rational* ;" and thus to bring about a final "*reconciliation*"
between "reason as self-conscious mind" and "reason as a given
reality."[2]

It is here that we face the most important consequence of the
total destruction of bourgeois evolutionary metaphysics which
is implied in Marx's materialistic criticism of the Hegelian
idealist dialectic. Marx's study of society is based upon a full
recognition of the *reality of historical change*. Marx treats all
conditions of existing bourgeois society as *changing* or, more
exactly, as conditions *being changed* by human actions. At the
same time, he regards all, even the most general categories of
social science, as categories changeable and *to be changed*. He
dismisses all the concepts applied by bourgeois social theorists
and historians, in which the present form of society is in any
way withdrawn from the constant flux of things, whether the
writer deals with present-day bourgeois conditions as "natural"
and as having always existed ; or whether, on the contrary, he
erects an impassable barrier between past social conditions and
the present-day bourgeois state of society ; or whether, again,
he recognizes a real change only with respect to previous history
and closes the whole development of human society with the
bourgeois state reached in the present age. Bourgeois society,
then, is no longer in any sense a general entity which can be
justified by another than the historical title. It is a transitory
stage which has been reached in the present time, and is valid

[1] See Hegel, *Encyclopædia*. I, addition to § 212.
[2] See Hegel, *Preface to Philosophy of Law* (1820).

temporarily for this particular epoch, yet to be replaced by another state in an historical movement. It is at the same time but the present result of an earlier phase, and the starting point of a new phase, of the social class struggle leading to a social revolution.

CHAPTER V

THE description of existing bourgeois conditions as *specific* conditions of a *transitory phase* in an historical process, assumes a further importance as a theoretical basis for a critical examination of the structure of present society as a particular historical type of socio-economic formation.

Just as in actual history every revolutionary movement of the bourgeoisie bred, as an undercurrent, independent stirrings of that class which was more or less the undeveloped predecessor of the modern proletariat, there have been even in the infancy of bourgeois thought some isolated thinkers who anticipated the criticism of the bourgeois principles which had not as yet been put into practice. Apart from these exceptional cases, a real theoretical understanding of the historical process and the self-criticism bound up with it did not arise in bourgeois thought until the very end of its classical epoch, when the revolutionary fight of the bourgeoisie against feudal society had come to its end and a new divergence of classes had begun to manifest itself within the hitherto united industrial society.

It was not a criticism, but in fact a glorification when, in the middle of the 17th century, Hobbes described the existing state of bourgeois society (or, as he imagined in conformity with the prevailing delusion of contemporary thinkers, of "society" in general) as a "bellum omnium contra omnes" or " a war of every man against every man," which is only effectively and finally brought to a close by "a common Power to keep them all in awe," i.e., by the iron dictatorship of the State. Again, it was a glorification of bourgeois society when, 50 years later, Mandeville spoke of its peculiar construction, purposely devised

57

by an "all-cunning" Providence, in his paradoxical equation "Private vices—public benefits." Once more, it was a glorification when, at the close of the 18th century, Kant discovered the "antagonism of unsocial sociality" by which eventually "the first true steps from uncouthness to culture, and the agreement to live in a society, are pathologically thrust upon man." "All culture and art which adorn mankind, the most beautiful social order, are fruits of that unsociality which by its own nature is compelled to discipline itself and thus fully to develop the germs of nature through an art forced upon it from without."[1]

While the Darwinian formula of a "*struggle for existence*" along with the older formula of Hobbes, had been misapplied by the eulogists of capitalism as a cosmic substructure of a so-called universal law of "free competition," Darwin himself had conversely borrowed his general concept from contemporary bourgeois economics. In the Introduction to the second edition of his famous work he said : "This is the doctrine of Malthus as applied to the whole realm of animal and plant life."[2] Indeed, the specific historical form of the division of labour which results from the competition of the isolated commodity producers within present bourgeois society is so far from being an unchangeable law of human nature that it can be best understood as a brute unconscious form of social self-preservation in contrast to the conscious organization of the division of labour within a really co-operative society. In that sense "civil society" had already been characteristically described by Hegel as a "geistiges Tierreich" ("the animal world reproduced in the world of the mind").[3] The analogy was further developed by Marx in *Capital* when he described the division of labour pre-

[1] See Hobbes, *Leviathan*, 1651; Mandeville, *The Fable of the Bees: Private Vices, Public Benefits*, 1706; Kant, *Idea of a Universal History Conceived under a Cosmopolitan Aspect*, 1784.
[2] See Darwin, *On the Origin of Species*, etc., second edition London, 1860. See also Marx, *Theories of Surplus Value*, II, i, p. 315.
[3] See Hegel, *Phenomenology of the Mind* (Sämtliche Werke, II, edition 1832, pp. 295-314).

vailing within present capitalistic society, as an organization which "confronts independent commodity producers one with another, who recognize no authority other than that of competition, that is, the coercion exercised upon them by the pressure of their reciprocal interests, *just as in the animal kingdom the 'war of all against all' maintains, more or less, the conditions of existence of all species.*"[1] It would be preferable, perhaps, in a strictly socio-economic research, to avoid altogether such parallels which never quite fit. However, the manner in which Darwin projects into nature, as an absolute law, the *Competitive Struggle* waged in bourgeois society, and in which Kropotkin equally unwarrantably transforms the opposite principle of co-operation prevailing in communist society into an absolute *Law of Mutual Help in the Animal and Human World*, are both quite different in calibre from the recent attempt by a former orthodox Marxist to project a self-invented pacifistic and evolutionary principle of a so-called *Natural Equilibrium* from present-day society, where it does not apply, to the whole animal and plant world, where it likewise does not apply.[2]

The fundamental weakness of all the more significant interpretations of society in this epoch (inclusive of Rousseau's teaching, the bourgeois novel of *Robinson Crusoe*, and the whole of the new bourgeois science of Political Economy) consists in the unhistorical manner in which they deal with the specific conditions of bourgeois society, its mode of production, its State, and its law, as final ; regarding them as a natural and rational society at last attained and now in its main features unchangeable or, what practically amounts to the same, as being capable of unlimited perfection. When Marx (in the "Seventh and last Observation" of his *Anti-Proudhon*) denounced this thoughtless procedure as applied by the economists, he hit the

[1] See *Capital*, I, p. 321.
[2] See Engels' letter to F. A. Lange, 11.3.65, and Marx's letter to Kugelmann, 27.6.70; see also the author's *Critical examination of the work of Karl Kautsky*, pp. 40 *et seq.*

whole school in the shrewd sentence, "Thus there was history, but there is no more."[1]

Thus bourgeois theorists have dealt with all earlier forms of society as barbaric preliminary stages leading up to their own, ultimately established civil society. This truly "barbaric" procedure was, according to Marx, unavoidable so long as their principal task consisted in fighting out their historical struggle with feudalism under the conditions of a bourgeois society not yet finally constituted. It served as a weapon in the battle for progress and did not need, as long as it still had a revolutionary spark in it, any further justification. It appears, from a historical viewpoint, as a last faint echo of those stronger, if more naïve, forms in which during the Peasant War and the English Revolution the "pre-history of humanity" pictured in the Bible and during the French Revolution the *natural state of man*, were opposed as a true civil state of society to the feudal and corrupted order of the middle ages. Those were revolutionary slogans of the new bourgeois class against feudalism.

> When Adam delved and Eve span
> Where was then the gentleman?

There was no such excuse for the further preservation of that antiquated method at a time when the victory of the bourgeois principle over feudalism had been finally won and the theorists of the triumphant bourgeoisie awoke to find themselves transformed unawares from revolutionary pioneers into the tedious panegyrists of an established order of society. Compare, for instance, the characteristic phraseology of the scientific founder of bourgeois "*Ideology*," Destutt de Tracy, who boasted that among the "Ancients" (i.e., in all epochs previous to the present "French Era") "social art" had not been sufficiently perfected "to give their empire that state of higher civilization and that strong organization which are necessary to secure the existence

[1] See *Misère de la Philosophie* (MEGA, I, vi, p. 188).

60

of nations effectively policed."[1] Or, compare those bourgeois historians of the French Restoration period in the 19th century who, like Guizot, Thiers, and Thierry, expressly set themselves the task of rewriting world history as the *history of the bourgeois class*.

In this phase the real progress of social science no longer consisted in the further development of bourgeois principles, but in their critique. The genuine self-criticism now for the first time arising within bourgeois science originated with the growth of classical political economy from *Adam Smith* to *Ricardo* and found its complete expression in the last phase of the development of classical German philosophy from *Kant* to *Hegel*.

Hegel's philosophical system is, as the last system of classical German philosophy, the sum and recapitulation not only of all the earlier phases of bourgeois social theory, but also of its inherent contradictions. Like Ricardo, the last classical writer in the field of economics, so Hegel in his philosophy brought into sharper relief the striking contrasts within the structure of civil society which had already been revealed to a certain extent by Mandeville, Ferguson, Adam Smith, Kant, etc., but which with them had been ultimately harmonized in some "higher" or "deeper" unity. Even Hegel, in dealing with the material conditions of existing society, nowhere passed beyond the range of bourgeois thought. Still this new world of the bourgeoisie with its internal oppositions ranging themselves like so many unbridgeable chasms, as it was now philosophically exposed by Hegel under the direct influence of Ricardo, stood in a striking contrast to that "best of all possible worlds" into which even the most daring among the bourgeois thinkers of the preceding generation had ideologically transfigured the hard facts of existing social life.

In Ricardo's economic system and in Hegel's philosophy,

[1] See *Eléments d'idéologie* (1800-1805), Vol. II, Introduction, p. 6.

bourgeois society reached the highest grade of critical self-consciousness of which it was capable without violating its own principles. This happened at a time when, in the most developed capitalistic countries such as England and France a "criticism from without" had opposed itself to bourgeois society in the growing revolt of the proletarian class. Just as the last classical economist (Ricardo) had already been faced by a consciously socialist critic of all bourgeois economic science (Sismondi), so Hegel reflected the tremors set up in his philosophical exposition of "civil society" under the foundations of bourgeois society by the new class of the hired labourers. He had realistically described this new "class" which had been brought into being by the bourgeoisie itself, as one "bound to the particular work of modern industry" and as one living "in need and dependence" and "excluded from all the advantages of bourgeois society;" as a "great mass" submerged below that "mode of subsistence" which is a necessary premise to the enjoyment of social rights, and sinking, by an inevitable law of bourgeois society itself, in the same proportion as the "excess of wealth" is increased into an increasing "excess of poverty."[1]

He furthermore accurately indicated that it is not a question here of "misery" alone, such as had inevitably arisen in earlier times through the parsimony of nature. It is a "social question" in the real sense of the term, pertinent to modern society, and one which must be solved by society. "No one can assert a right against nature, but, in the state of society, the defect takes at once the form of an injustice inflicted on one or the other class. The important question as to how poverty is to be relieved is one which particularly agitates and annoys society."[2] He described in characteristic language the "temper" of the great masses of industrial workers which is inseparably bound up with the socially inflicted poverty in which they are forced to live.

[1] See Hegel, *Philosophy of Law*, §§ 243-45.
[2] *Ibid.*, addition to § 244.

"It is," he says, "an inner revolt against the rich, against society, against the government, etc."[1]

The impassable limit for Hegel, as for all other social scientists of the bourgeoisie, consisted in the fact that he saw the new social class only negatively as the "mob," and did not realize at the same time its positive revolutionary implications.[2]

Even more distinctly than in its contents, the critical element inherent in Hegel's philosophy manifests itself in his *method*. Hegel, unlike Ricardo, had not contented himself with stating the fundamental "principles" and letting the most glaring theoretical discordances stand as so-called "modifications." He endeavoured to confine within one philosophical system, both the given condition of the existing bourgeois State and what he called its "idea." The "dialectical method" is the great instrument by which Hegel in his philosophy, complying with the needs of a class pressing toward the termination of the revolutionary movement and to a political and social "restoration," performed the remarkable task of reconciling within a so-called "unity of contradictions," the most irreconcilable oppositions resulting from the historical development of bourgeois society itself, and from its later confrontation with the rising class of the proletarian wage-labourers. Whilst his basic description of the existing conditions of "civil society," though suffering from vagueness, abruptness, and arbitrary judgments, still contains the deep insight of a genius fully aware of bourgeois reality, the cloven foot of his philosophy unequivocally reveals itself in the "speculative" super-structure of Hegel's system, which, in an apparent endeavour to establish a new idealistic creed corresponding to the needs of the present time, actually restores the

[1] See Hegel, *Philosophy of Law*, addition to § 244.
[2] See MEGA, I, iii, pp. 204-208. While here Marx, quite correctly, confronted the restricted view-point of his former companions of the road among the "left" Hegelians, who had not gone beyond Hegel's bourgeois suggestions, with the revolutionary implications of the proletarian class struggle set forth by such contemporary writers as Proudhon, some years later he, less appropriately, raised the same point against Proudhon himself in *Misère de la philosophie* (MEGA, I, vi, p. 191).

whole bulk of old mediæval metaphysics—inclusive of the Christian dogma—which had been so utterly refuted by the spokesmen of early bourgeois materialism in the intervening centuries of progressive bourgeois thought.[1]

This Hegelian method, which had proved so efficient in swallowing the most powerful contradictions, offered no small temptation to the generation of radical thinkers which arose in the period immediately following Hegel's death, when the unchallenged sway of Hegelian philosophy preceded, during the 30's and 40's of the 19th century, the final decline of the Hegelian and, indeed, all bourgeois philosophy.[2] They thought that the mighty instrument, forged by the last great philosopher of the bourgeois class, could easily be made available for the more advanced criticism raised against the very principle of the bourgeois status quo in the name of the new revolutionary class. All that was needed was to consider the "premature" termination of Hegel's philosophy in the glorification of the bourgeois society, its State, its philosophy, its religion and art, to be only an "inconsistency," on the part of the conservative "systematizer," in the application of his own revolutionary "method." In fact Lassalle—and Proudhon for a time—did assign this new historical task to Hegel's dialectical method.

Marx and Engels saw clearly that the old bottle could no longer hold the new wine. It is true that they too, in the formation of their new proletarian and materialistic criticism of bourgeois society, took their departure from Hegel's idealistic philosophy and even preserved the term "Dialectic" as a comprehensive name for the several new principles which they worked out and applied in the process of their scientific investigation. But, as will be shown in the third part of this book, all that apparent "Hegelianism" did not amount, in Marx, to more

[1] See the author's *Theses on Hegel and the Revolution*, published on the 100th anniversary of Hegel's death (1931) in German and French periodicals.
[2] For a more detailed description of this period see the author's *Marxism and Philosophy*, second edition, 1930.

than what he at one time most appropriately called an "occasional flirtation with Hegel's peculiar mode of expression."[1] In actual fact, he completely broke with the whole of Hegel's speculative philosophy. He transplanted the dialectical method of Hegel from an idealistic to a materialistic basis, and in the process of that materialistic "reversal" stripped from it all those elements which he had already thoroughly exposed in an earlier phase of his philosophical development as its underlying "mystification."[2] The theory of the new revolutionary movement of the 19th century no longer needed to exercise itself in the art of moving forward and backward at the same time, and to represent its new aims as the "restoration" of the old. It "left the dead to bury their dead" in order to come to its own content.[3]

The principles of the Marxian critique of existing society, being proletarian and no longer bourgeois, are opposed to the philosophical system of Hegel not only in content, subject matter, and aim, but quite as much in theoretical form. If Marx, indeed, took his start from a critical and revolutionary reversal of the principles inherent in Hegel's method, he certainly went on to develop, in a strictly empirical manner, the specific methods of his own materialistic criticism and research.

There is, aside from the theoretical self-criticism of bourgeois society represented by the later classical writers, another, and entirely different, criticism which flows from the latter of the two above-mentioned currents of 19th century bourgeois thought[4] and which, this time, is directed against the very principle of theoretical analysis itself. Marx, from his new standpoint, saw at once the real character of the *Historico-Romantic School* which after the close of the great French Revolution had

[1] See *Postscript*, 1873.
[2] See Marx's "critical revision" of Hegel's *Philosophy of Law*, 1843, in MEGA, I, 1, i, pp. 401-453, and the reference to that earlier analysis in *Postscript*, 1873.
[3] See Marx, *The 18th Brumaire of Louis Bonaparte*, 1852.
[4] See above, p. 45.

joined, and even in part preceded, the socialists in the attack upon the victorious bourgeois principles. He disclosed in his article on *The Philosophical Manifesto of the Historical School of Law*,[1] and in the analysis of "Reactionary Socialism" embodied in the *Communist Manifesto*, the essentially reactionary trend of that apparently "anti-bourgeois" and "anti-capitalistic" current which—like reactionary Fascism and Hitlerism to-day—"upbraided the bourgeoisie more for having produced a *revolutionary* proletariat than for having produced a proletariat at all."[2] He has also seen the theoretical loss bound up with this sentimental regression from the only present and real form of social life to mediæval feudality and even further back to archaic conditions of society,—the so-called "origins" of culture, art, economics, etc. "The Historical School," jests Marx, "has so emphasized its affection for 'sources', that it requires the sailor to sail, not on the stream but on its source."[3]

While thus refuting the entire theoretical and practical "philosophy" of the Historical School, in agreement with all progressive spirits of the age,[4] Marx was at the same time aware of the actual progress which had been made by this new school of social research from a purely scientific point of view. Moreover, he discovered the critical and forward tendency inherent in the apparently backward turn. Writing to Engels on the 25th of March, 1868, he said : "The first reaction against the French Revolution and the 'enlightenment' bound up with it was,

[1] See MEGA, I, 1, i, pp. 251 *et seq.*
[2] *Ibid*, I, vi, p. 547.
[3] *Ibid*, I, 1, i, p. 251.
[4] See the report in MEGA, I, 1, i, pp. XLIX-L, on the four essays by which young Marx in 1842 intended to refute the several aspects of the Historico-Romantic School. See also the vigorous indictment, in MEGA, I, v, p. 325, of such forerunners of that school as the first French theorists of the counter-revolution, Bonald, de Maistre, etc., and their followers during the French Restoration—the real founders of all later "Tory-Socialism." The same people are referred to in the *Communist Manifesto* as a section of the French Legitimists and of "Young England" who "waved the proletarian alms-bag in front for a banner but carried the old feudal coat-of-arms on their hindquarters." (MEGA, I, vi, p. 547.)

naturally, to see everything as mediæval and romantic. Even such writers as Grimm are not free from this. The second reaction is to see beyond the Middle Ages back into the primitive history of each people. That corresponds to the socialist view, although the scholars have no idea of the connection. Thus they are surprised to find the newest in the oldest, and even 'Egalitarians,' to a degree which would scandalize Proudhon."[1]

From this sentence, to which a hundred similar ones might be added from Marx's and Engels' writings, can be seen the main significance that the study of primæval society, then passing through its first great period of discovery, had at that time acquired for the revolutionary science of Marx.[2] The very fact that now, for the first time, those social forms of existence which hitherto had been so far removed from present-day conditions and had been accessible to the modern world at best in legend and poetry were opened up to sober scientific research, was for Marx and Engels a sign that bourgeois society in its present stage of development already contained within itself the tendencies toward a change more radical than any achieved by previous historical revolutions. The basic importance of primitive history rests on this general assumption rather than on the analogy which Marx, half in joke, draws between the "egalitarian" conditions of primæval society and the communist society of the future.

While the term of "primæval communism," created by the first discoverers, has since been rather indiscriminately applied to the various types of early society, there still remains a striking, and even somewhat paradoxical, difference between the bourgeois and the Marxian use of the underlying concept. The idea of an historical past repeating itself in the future fits in very well with the bourgeois concept of development, with its glorification of existing bourgeois conditions, and with its rejection of "communism" as implying a general loss of culture and an

[1] See MEGA, III, iv, p. 33.　　　　[2] See above, p. 50.

eventual relapse from the present "all time high" of human achievement to primitive barbarism and decay. On the other hand, the assumption that Marx and Engels should have seen in the conditions prevailing in a distant past an actual anticipation of conditions to be reached in an equally distant future, and thus reduced the Communist programme to a mere restoration of that long bygone past, utterly contradicts the materialistic principle underlying the whole of Marxian theory. Marx presents human society as an historical development progressing from a lower to a higher organization of the material productive forces. He sees in the modern capitalistic mode of production, with its immense unfolding of productive powers far exceeding all earlier epochs, an indispensable material foundation for that more highly developed form of communal life which will be inaugurated by the social revolution of the modern working class.

Nevertheless, many bourgeois writers up to the present day, after a perfunctory recital of the well-known theoretical unsoundness of the assumption of a "Primæval Communism," and after a scholarly refutation of the historical mistakes allegedly committed in this respect by the Marxists, quite naïvely go on to make use of the term and its underlying assumption. On the contrary, the idea of a primitive "Communism" preceding the various systems based on private property is openly accepted from the outset by the Marxists but at the same time is nowhere used by them as an argument for a positive historical statement. It serves them rather as a starting point for a more thorough and more critical investigation of the given conditions of existing society including even its most far-reaching and, from a less comprehensive view-point, remote developmental tendencies.

There is then, from the very principle of Marxian materialistic research, a great significance in the investigation of the primitive conditions prevailing in the early history of mankind. Yet this investigation is made by the Marxists, not for the purpose of acquiring a direct knowledge of the really communistic forms and contents of a future, post-capitalist society, but rather with the indirect aim of a more comprehensive approach to the study of historical change. Marx and Engels saw in the scientific unfolding of primæval history a necessary premise for their materialistic investigation of present-day society, whose basic forms can only be fully elucidated by an exact study of primitive society, its development and dissolution, and the different forms of its transition to the later systems based on private property and class opposition. For example, in order to explain scientifically the surviving remains of communal property and the various original types of private property in the Greek, Roman, Germanic, Celtic, and Slavonic social systems, it is necessary to go back to the various forms of primitive communal property and the corresponding different forms of their dissolution.

Besides this main interest, there are some other advantages to be gained from that source for a critical and revolutionary science. The critical science of the proletarian class was the first to break loose from the accepted single track idea of progress, and to show that those apparently "wild" and "barbaric" conditions of the primæval past, in spite of their material deficiencies, uncouthness, and benightedness, still contained many qualities which compare most favourably with present-day "civilized" conditions. Marx and Engels in that respect only continued, and in a more highly developed form, the "criticism of civilization" which had been initiated before them by the first great Utopian socialists, above all by Charles Fourier in his vital attack on the self-complacent assurance of the bourgeois conception of the world.[1] It is only with a knowledge of the totally non-bourgeois forms of a primitive society that it becomes possible for the social revolutionary to imagine a further development

[1] See Engels, *Origin of the Family, Private Property, and the State,* 1884, where Fourier's profound discernment of the contrast between civilized society and the primitive forms is recapitulated in a footnote to the penultimate paragraph. The theme is further elaborated in Engels' *Anti-Dühring,* 1878, and in his *Preface* to the fourth edition of *Origin,* etc., in 1891.

which will go beyond the bourgeois conditions of present-day society not only by a gradual readjustment of its existing pattern but by a fundamental change of the whole system. The communist societies of the future will, in proportion to their increasing distance from the present-day bourgeois status, "correspond," no longer merely to Mediæval and Antique Society, but to a still further distant and entirely non-bourgeois past. They will not conform, however, to those early conditions commonly referred to as Primitive Communism in any other way than in their analogous position "equally aloof from present-day society." There need be, in fact, as little structural likeness between those primæval conditions of humanity (or for that matter the equally "primitive" conditions of the so-called "savage" tribes to-day) and the future conditions of a fully developed communist society, as there is at the present time between the "unconscious" elements of the mental structure of modern bourgeois man as recently disclosed by the psychoanalysts on the one hand, and the "corresponding" states of either primæval man or the free individuals of a no longer bourgeois society of the future.

The occurrence of a genuine critical impulse in the history of bourgeois social thought, then, is restricted to a short and clearly defined period. It emerged from the last phase of the revolutionary epoch of the bourgeoisie, and it ended with the expiration of this, the "classical" epoch of bourgeois social science. As we shall show in detail in the second part of this book, none of the post-classical schools of bourgeois economists has even approximated the critical detachment which, for a strictly limited time, had been reached by such thinkers as Ricardo. The same applies to the post-Hegelian developments of bourgeois philosophy and, indeed, to all other branches of post-classical bourgeois thought, even though more recently its hitherto prevailing tendency to accept unconditionally or to defend and glorify existing conditions has been overshadowed, in some cases, by the apparent counteraction of a directly opposite tendency.

The vehement protests raised from time to time by otherwise well-disposed critics against some particularly disgraceful aspects of the existing social order, the occasional lapses of an exceptionally impressionable literatus into an entire negation of present society, and the equivalent pessimistic, ironic, or sceptical currents in contemporary bourgeois philosophy do not initiate a new phase in the development of modern social thought. All these apparent expressions of an enhanced bourgeois "self-criticism," varying from the Freudian scientific analysis of the *Civilization and its Discontents*, to the inflation of such minor "discontents" into a *Decline of the West*, or a final *Breakdown* of Modern Civilization,[1] rather serve the purpose of opening an illusory outlet to the feelings aroused in the lower strata of the bourgeoisie by their increasingly oppressed condition, or to the temporary hangovers befalling the entire class under the impact of a defeat in war or of a major economic depression.

Such ideological phenomena, while purporting to express an increasing critical self-consciousness of bourgeois society, indicate only an increasing unwillingness on the part of the hitherto ruling class to understand its own social mode of existence as a specific entity.

The essential futility of every attempt of contemporary bourgeois self-criticism appears most strikingly in the ideological repercussions, resulting from the periodic cycle through which modern industry runs. The alternate occurrence of an absolute denial and an equally absolute acceptance of the *universal crisis*, periodically repeating itself in the theory of bourgeois economists, along with the periodical recurrence of prosperity and depression, can best be regarded as being itself a secondary phenomenon of a given phase of the industrial cycle. The fact

[1] Titles of recent books by Freud, Spengler, Briffault.

that bourgeois economists have not yet arrived at a "theory of the crisis," independent of the momentary fluctuations of the industrial process, only emphasizes once more *a definite incapacity of present-day bourgeois society to grasp "specifically" the process of its own destruction.*

A critical investigation of the existing conditions of mankind which conceives of the imminent break-down of existing bourgeois conditions not as an absolute disintegration but as a *transition from the present historical phase to a higher form of society* can only be attempted and carried through in an unbiassed and consistent manner by the *new social class produced by the bourgeoisie itself.*

CHAPTER VI

BEFORE we deal with the practical implications of Marx's critical investigation of existing bourgeois society, we shall discuss a strictly theoretical problem arising from the statements made in the preceding chapters with regard to the main methodological principles of Marxian science. How does that emphasis on "specification," which we have shown to be the very foundation of Marx's materialistic criticism and research, conform to the equally fundamental demand for some degree of generalization which is necessarily bound up with every attempt at a truly scientific statement, and is certainly recognized by Marx.

As shown in the second and third chapters, Marx scornfully dismissed the superficial and arbitrary procedure of the bourgeois social scientists who described the various conditions of different historical stages in the terms of the same general concepts and thus "by a sleight of hand represented bourgeois conditions as unchangeable natural laws pertaining to society *in abstracto*."[1] He was equally critical of that complete abstention from all theoretical generalization which is the idea vaguely aimed at by the Historical School and other irrationalists. As against both, he worked out a new type of generalization.

Here again, Marx took his departure from the work of the idealistic philosopher Hegel. This latter too had rejected the abstractual procedure commonly applied by the social theorists as well as what he called the "conceptlessness" underlying the historical trends of the early 19th century. In opposition to both, he had posed another principle : That of the "truly general."[2] The "general" as it appears in the most developed forms of

[1] See above, pp. 24 *et seq.*
[2] See Hegel, *Encyclopædia*, I, § 163, and *Philosophy of Law* § 24.

73

philosophical thought is, according to Hegel's terminology, dialectically identical with the "particular" and, indeed, with "individual existence." Or, as this Hegelian principle has been most succinctly recapitulated in a single sentence : "*Truth is concrete.*"

Of course, this highly paradoxical formula had not yet acquired with the idealistic philosopher that unequivocally realistic connotation which it was to assume later with Marx and such other dialectic materialists as Engels, Antonio Labriola, Plechanov, and Lenin. The new emphasis laid by Hegel on the subject matter of human thought as against its mere form was not meant as a materialistic adherence to the given external facts, but rather served as a starting point for a new and more refined form of the most daring philosophical abstraction. Philosophical thought, according to Hegel, is no more to be regarded as being a mere reflection, in the mind of the philosopher, of the concrete facts of an external world. It is, on the contrary, understood to be the most concrete existence itself, and to comprise within itself both the abstract concepts formed as a first approach to truth in ordinary practical and theoretical human thought, and the equally "abstract" forms of externally given "concrete" realities.

Hegel's "concrete," then, by no means coincides with the sensually concrete of given experience and practical action. Factual knowledge was for him a means rather than an end. A faithful acceptance of the empirical data of nature and history was to prepare the ground for an idealistic reconstruction of the universe and thus to testify once more to the absolute precedence of the conceptual form over all external existence.

Thus the real meaning of the Hegelian "concrete" was somewhat one-sidedly interpreted by that remarkable series of theoretical and practical leaders of the revolutionary proletarian movement beginning with Lassalle and ending with Lenin who looked at Hegel's philosophy as an essentially empirical method of thought. The irremovable ambiguity pervading the whole of the Hegelian philosophy affects also his apparently realistic approach to "the concrete." If on the one hand he conceived of the philosophical idea as something other than an empty form and defined it as "that which is the concrete itself," he was equally ready to explain that he did not understand by the concrete "what is commonly understood by this term," but merely the speculative "concrete" resulting from idealistic philosophical thought.

The theorists of abstraction proceeded to the formation of their general concepts by starting from the concrete of common experience and getting rid of its particular qualities by a method of successive elimination. The *irrationalists* believed that they could get hold of the concrete in an immediate manner. *Hegel* fancied that in his philosophy he had reached the concrete truth of the idea by starting from a first general concept and supplying the details by a successive adoption of the particular results of scientific research and historical development. *Marx* was the first to work out a rational type of generalization, different from the traditional conceptual procedures hitherto applied by the various schools of social, historical and philosophical thought, and more akin to the constructive procedures recently invented by the experimental scientists. With him, as shown by the examples discussed in the second and third chapters of this book, the "general" of the concept is no longer set up against concrete reality as another realm ; but every "general," even in its conceptual form, necessarily remains a specific aspect or a mentally dissected part of the historical concrete of existing bourgeois society.[1]

Thus the unconscious and half-hearted self-criticism of bourgeois social science which had previously made its appearance in the Historical School and in Hegel, was finally transformed, by Marx, into an attack against both the ideas and the existence

[1] See above, p. 29 *et seq.*

of the bourgeois order. The fixed abstractions of bourgeois science, which had long since ceased to serve as tools of a truly progressive thought and had degenerated into fetters upon the further advance of social knowledge, were now confronted with their present *concrete* existence. Hence, the previously established status of modern "civilized" society was deprived of its false halo ; and its underlying prose, the real conditions of life under capitalistic rule, could be freely contrasted with the germs of a new proletarian mode of existence. The "concrete," i.e., the real, social, economic, and class *contents* of existing society were confronted with their abstract conceptual *form*, and the as yet *unformed* substance of a new proletarian socialist and communist "becoming" was opposed to the *fully determined* forms of existing bourgeois "being." This is *one* of the "materialistic" tendencies of the new, revolutionary science of society.

While bourgeois science defines the *wealth* of society as the "wealth of nations"[1] or a "general property"[2], and the *State* as a form of unity necessary for society, Marx does not deny the "abstract" truth of such statements. He simply adds that, under the prevailing "concrete" conditions, the wealth of a nation is the *capital* of the ruling bourgeois class and that, in the same way, the present bourgeois State is the *political form of the rule of the bourgeoisie over the proletarian class*. In the same way, Marx does not question the "abstract" proposition that "all combined labour on a large scale, both in capitalist and socialist production, requires *a directing authority*, in order to secure the necessary harmony among the individual activities and to perform the general functions arising from the movement of the whole productive body as distinguished from the movements of its independent organs."[3] He merely calls attention to the exploitation and despotism which the *capitalistic direction of the social*

[1] See the title of Adam Smith's economic work: *An Inquiry into the Nature and Causes of the "Wealth of Nations."*
[2] See Hegel, *Encyclopædia*, III, § 524, and *Philosophy of Law*, § 199-200.
[3] See *Capital*, I, p. 295.

labour process inflicts upon the wage-labourers subordinated to it, under the prevailing social conditions. While the bourgeois apologists compare the function of modern capitalistic management with that of the conductor of an orchestra, Marx compares the concrete forms in which, under fully developed capitalistic conditions, the command over the mass of workmen collaborating in a workshop is exercised in the name of the absentee owner through a whole hierarchy of managers, foremen, overlookers, etc., with the command of an army through its commissioned and non-commissioned officers. In spite of the apparent "freedom" of the labour contract there is, from a social point of view, no voluntary self-subordination of the army of workers to a supreme leadership necessary for the common good. "The capitalist is not a capitalist because he is a leader of industry. He becomes a commander of industry because he is a capitalist. Supreme command in industry is an attribute of capital, just as, in feudal times, supreme command in war and in the courts of justice was an attribute of the landed proprietor."[1] Moreover, such uniformity of command exists in bourgeois society only for the single workshop within a system of social production which as a whole, is neither planned nor directed, and barely balanced subsequently only by the competitive struggle of individual commodity producers. As a general rule, there is even an inverse relation between the authority exercised within the single workshop and the existence of a planned co-operation within the whole of a given capitalistic society. It is precisely the people most loudly extolling the wholesome results of an unconditional subordination of individual workers to the capitalistic "organization of labour," who denounce equally loudly every kind of deliberate control and regulation of the social process of production as an invasion of the inviolable property rights, liberty, and self-determining "genius" of the individual capitalist. "It is characteristic that the enthusiastic apologists of

[1] See *Capital*, I, p. 297.

77

the factory system can find nothing worse to say against every general organization of co-operative work, than that it would transform the whole of society into a factory."[1] This whole process of confronting the abstract bourgeois concepts of State and Authority with the actual facts of the master and servant relationship growing directly out of the present-day form of capitalistic production, ultimately resolves itself into a transition to the new form of socialist production just struggling into being. While in bourgeois society the dead accumulated labour of the past rules as "capital" over present living labour, in communist society conversely, the accumulated labour of past generations will be but a means to widen, to enrich, and to further the existence of the workers.[2]

While the bourgeois social theorists, with so-called "general" concepts framed according to their usual abstractual procedure, ended by not grasping any real historical stage of social development at all, Marx, by his rational use of a new theoretical procedure conceived on the model of the dialectical principle of Hegelian philosophy, arrived at the unique form of *generalization*, which is in keeping with the most fully developed methods of modern experimental science. Bourgeois "sociologists," who apparently are concerned with society in general, remain entwined in the particular categories of bourgeois society. Marx, by analyzing the specific historical form of bourgeois society, attains a general knowledge of a social development far transcending that particular form. While the bourgeois theorists endeavour to proceed to an abstract general concept of "society" by a successive elimination of more and more empirically (i.e.,

[1] See *Capital*, I, p. 321.
[2] See *Communist Manifesto* (MEGA, I, vi, p. 540). On the whole question of authority see Marx: *Misère de la Philosophie* (MEGA, I, vi, pp. 198 *et seq.*); *Capital*, I, pp. 294 *et seq.*, 321 *et esq.*; *Capital*, III, ii, pp. 324-25, 418; Engels: *Eugen Dühring's Revolution of Science*, and his article *Dell' autorità* in *Publicazione della Plebe*, Lodi, 1873. See further Lenin: *State and Revolution* August-September, 1917), and *Next Tasks of the Soviet Power*, Report delivered at the session of the All-Russian Central Executive Committee of Workmen's, Soldiers', Peasants' and Cossacks' Delegates, 29.4.1918.

historically) given data of bourgeois society, and thus often unconsciously retain just those features which happen to be the most singular ones, Marx is aware of the fact that the only possible way of comprehending the general concept, or the "law," of a particular historical form of society is through its actual historical change. Modern natural science no longer employs the old scholastic Aristotelian method. It no longer bases its generalizations upon an arbitrarily chosen common feature of a given number of objects which is thus constituted as a class of such objects. For instance, it does not proceed from the observation of falling stones to a general law of the fall of stones. It proceeds from the analysis of a single case observed in all its particularity, or rather from a single experiment carried out under exactly determined conditions, to formulate the general law of gravity which now, under varying conditions with correspondingly varying results, applies alike to falling stones, to stones at rest, and also to such other things as balloons, planets and comets. In the same manner an exact social science cannot form its *general concepts* by the simple abstraction of certain more or less arbitrarily chosen traits of the given historical form of bourgeois society. It must secure the knowledge of the general contained in that particular form of society by the exact investigation of all the historical conditions underlying its emergence from another state of society and by the actual modification of its present form under exactly established conditions. Only thus can social research be transformed into an exact science based upon observation and experiment.

Just as in modern natural science the general law has no independent existence outside the collection of the particular cases covered by its application, so the social law exists only in the historical development through which a particular form of society proceeds from its particular state in the past to its particular state in the present and from that to the social forms brought about by its further change. Thus the only genuine laws in social science are the laws of historical change. The Russian reviewer of *Capital*,[1] whose statements are quoted in part and adopted by Marx in the *Postscript* to the second edition, has most aptly brought out this realistic principle of the new Marxian science. He shows that Marx, in spite of the outward form of his presentation which, according to the reviewer, is "idealistic" in the German, i.e., the bad, sense of the term, "is in actual fact enormously more of a realist than any of his predecessors in the realm of economic criticism." Whereas in idealistic philosophical thought as well as in the ordinary abstract way of scientific thinking, the facts of a particular social state are compared with some "idea," Marx's criticism confronts a given fact "not with the idea, but only with another fact," and so, by the most exact possible study of each fact, represents the facts themselves as "different momenta of a development" confronting one another. While the old economists set up abstract general laws of economic life which were expected to apply equally to the past, the present, and the future, no such general laws of economic life are conformable to the principle of historical change, as established by Marx.

In his opinion, on the contrary, every historical period has laws peculiar to itself. . . . As soon as life has gone through a given period of development and is passing over from one given stage to another, it begins also to be controlled by other laws. . . . Nay, more, one and the same phenomenon is subject to entirely different laws as a result of the difference in the general structure of the social organisms replacing each other in the historical process, of the variation of their various organs, of the difference in the conditions under which they function, etc. Marx denies, for example, that the law of population is one and the same for all periods and all places. He contends, on the contrary, that every stage of development has its own law of population. . . . As productive powers move on in their development, so do social conditions and the laws gov-

[1] See I. I. Kaufmann in *Petersburg European Messenger*, 1872.

erning them change. While Marx sets himself the task of investigating and explaining the capitalistic economic order from this standpoint, he merely outlines in strictly scientific terms the aim that every exact investigator of economic conditions must have in view. . . . The scientific value of such research lies in the disclosure of the particular laws which control the origin, existence, development, and death of a given social organism and its replacement by another and higher one. Such, indeed, is the value of Marx's book.

CHAPTER VII

CONNECTION with a practical social movement is not peculiar to the Marxian theory. Bourgeois theory of society as well, in all its phases, has served a definite practical purpose. In its classical period it served the aims of the rising industrial class struggling for the theoretical and practical supremacy of the new bourgeois principles over the obsolete forms of feudal society. Later, after the victory of the bourgeois principles, bourgeois social thought split into parts. Its main current took to defending the established rule of the bourgeois class against the now rising proletarian class, and for this purpose posed as a "pure" and assumedly "unbiassed" science. Another current, following a tendency already visible in Comte, elaborated a more or less consciously counter-revolutionary set of ideas, foreshadowing the political programmes which were later to be adopted and put into practice by such movements as Italian Fascism and German National Socialism.

The only point which distinguishes the Marxist theory is that it represents the interests of *another* class and that it is *conscious* of its class character in a rational way, and not only in the delusive manner of a fascist or national socialist "mythology." "The theoretical propositions of the Communists express merely, in general terms, actual conditions of an existing class struggle, or of an historical movement going on under our very eyes." The representatives of liberal and democratic bourgeois science who naively assumed that this statement of the *Communist Manifesto*[1] implied a surrender, on the part of the Marxists, of the claim to the theoretical truth of their ideas, resemble the theologians who

[1] See MEGA I, vi, p. 538.

regard every religion but theirs as the invention of men and only their own as a divine revelation. Materialistic criticism, which defines all theoretical truths as mere historical "forms of social consciousness," does in no way abandon the quest for theoretical truth, but only replaces the traditional concept of an absolute truth by a less ambitious and much more practical idea. Every truth, according to the Marxists, applies only to a definite set of conditions ; it is therefore not absolute but relative, not independent and complete in itself, but contingent upon external facts. To-day's truth, then, depends upon the existing mode of material production and the class struggle arising therefrom. But this new definition of truth in no way lessens, nay, it enhances, the strictness of the formal demands which must be fulfilled by a "true" proposition from the standpoint of materialistic science.

What goes on here is only a repetition of the same process by which in the beginnings of bourgeois society, at first in the struggle of lay thought against the theological and metaphysical system of the Middle Ages, then in that of empiricism against all metaphysics, present-day "bourgeois" science was created. On the very threshold of the new age, Bacon, in his *Novum Organum*, which was to assist the emerging bourgeois science in the assertion of its new methods of empirical research, proclaimed the historical character of every science : "*Recte enim veritas temporis filia dicitur non auctoritatis.*"[1] On that authority of all authorities, Time, he based the superiority of the finally emancipated new science as against the dogmatic tenets of mediæval authorities.

This time, however, the proposed change of traditional historical form of consciousness reaches further, and by an apparently reversionary movement the very "freedom" and "independence" which was the boast of bourgeois philosophy and science during the intervening epoch of its almost unchallenged

[1] See Book I, 84.

supremacy, is now called in question again. Not only are the theological and metaphysical creeds which had been re-accepted by the bourgeoisie in a remodelled form now utterly "debunked," but also the new philosophy of the bourgeois era, and the whole body of its new historical and social truths, are finally stripped of their imaginary independence and drawn into the flux of things and the torment of the battle. Unconditional "this-sidedness," and a distinct historical and class character, become essential attributes not only of the *contents*, but also of the *form* of knowledge. This applies even to the revolutionary theory itself. The Marxian theory, which deals with all ideas as being connected with a definite historical epoch and the specific form of society pertaining to that epoch, recognizes itself as being just as much an historical product as any other theory pertaining to a definite stage of social development and to a definite social class. Thus the new science of the proletariat breaks with the last "ideological" limitations which had still hampered the critical self-consciousness of social science, and by reason of which the bourgeois investigators had imagined that, because their science had been freed from the specific fetters of mediæval dogma and metaphysics, it had become, once for all, a "free science," standing "above" the antagonisms of the new social order and of the pressure of vested interests.

The materialistic theory of the historical development of society is a particular form of the social consciousness of the present epoch and thus is itself a part of that historical development. The materialistic theory of the class struggle is itself class struggle. The materialistic theory of the social revolution of the proletarian class is at the same time a powerful lever in that same social revolution.

Thus amplified, all examples we have hitherto given to illustrate the critical and revolutionary functions of the materialistic theory, gain a new and enhanced significance.

If the materialistic science of society treats such subjects of

84

social investigation as *State* and *law*, (seemingly "above class"), in their specific historical character, i.e., as a State for the bourgeoisie and a law against the proletariat, it does not enunciate a pure theoretical proposition which may incidentally furnish a suitable argument for the practical attacks of the proletariat against existing bourgeois institutions. There is a much closer connection between the theoretical contents and the practical implications of the Marxian statement, for the two are, in fact, but related aspects of one single whole. The same applies to Marx's specific description of social *wealth* as "bourgeois wealth," i.e., as a collection of "commodities," which are not produced because they are useful, but because of the value and surplus value they contain ; or again, as the wealth of the capitalist class from which the proletariat is excluded ; or as capitalistic plenty and proletarian poverty ; or, finally, as the capitalist's own property (*"Eigentum"*) which for the proletariat (to use an apt expression of Lassalle's) is for ever but "the other man's property" (*"Fremdtum"*). It also applies to *material production*, now considered in its specific character as a "capitalistic commodity production," i.e., as an apparent activity of capital "breeding surplus value," behind which is hidden the real exploitation of the actual producers by the monopolistic owners of the social means of production : and so on, through the whole series of economic, political, legal, cultural, and other bourgeois categories.

It is also much more than a mere progress of theoretical knowledge when the materialistic theory, by its consistent application of the *principle of change*, immerses each and every social entity in the flux of an historical transition and thus reinterprets all static concepts of things in terms of so many dynamic processes and of an historical struggle between the social classes.

By this process of an historical specification of all bourgeois institutions, and by insistence on the constant working of change, materialistic science achieves in a theoretical way what is achieved in practice by the real historical movement of the proletariat. Thus Marx's materialistic social research though not for a moment abandoning its character of a strictly theoretical science, yet consciously assumes its particular function within the whole of a movement striving to transform existing society, and thus constitutes itself as a necessary part of the revolutionary action of the modern working class.

The ruling classes deny the scientific character of Marxism because of its class limitations. Marxism bases the wider and deeper truth of its propositions on its proletarian class character.

Marxian theory, viewed in its general character, is a new science of bourgeois society. It appears at a time when within bourgeois society itself, an independent movement of a new social class is opposing the ruling bourgeois class. In opposition to the bourgeois principles it represents the new views and claims of the class oppressed in bourgeois society. It is, so far, not a positive but a critical science. It "specifies" bourgeois society and investigates the tendencies visible in the present development of society, and the way to its imminent practical transformation. Thus it is not only a theory of bourgeois society but, at the same time, a theory of the proletarian revolution.

PART TWO
POLITICAL ECONOMY

CHAPTER I

MARXISM AND POLITICAL ECONOMY

MARX'S materialistic investigation of bourgeois society is based from the very beginning on a recognition of the cardinal importance of Political Economy. While but a few weeks before, he had written to his bourgeois-democratic friend Ruge, the characteristic words that the critic of modern society may start from "any given form of theoretical and practical consciousness" and that more especially the "political State" expresses within its form all social struggles, needs, and truths *sub specie rei publicae*,[1] he now definitely transcended that intermediate stage of his materialistic moulding process by the conclusion that "the anatomy of civil society must be sought for in Political Economy."[2] Nor was this merely an advance toward a better method of scientific investigation. The theoretical transition to Political Economy coincided with a practical transition from the Jacobinic bourgeois revolution, which had aimed at solving the social problems and needs of the working classes *sub specie rei publicae*, to the independent action of the modern proletariat, which is resolved to seek for the specific roots of its oppression and for the specific path to its emancipation in Political Economy. "The economic emancipation of the working class," say the Rules of the Working Men's International

[1] See Marx's letter to Ruge, dated "September 1843," as reproduced in the *Correspondence of 1843*, published in *Deutsch-Franzoesische Jahrbuecher*, 1844 (now reprinted MEGA I, 1, i, p. 574).

[2] See above, p. 20. For the first expression of this new materialistic knowledge, still philosophical in form, refer to the concluding paragraphs of Marx's *Introduction to a Critique of the Hegelian Philosophy of Law*, written in December, 1843 (MEGA, I, 1, i, pp. 619 *et seq.*), and for its further development to Marx's *Marginal Notes to Ruge's article "The King of Prussia and Social Reform,"* 1844, in which he finally confronted the political idealism of the most advanced wing of the revolutionary bourgeoisie, as represented by Ruge, with the economic and materialistic viewpoint of the proletarian class (MEGA, I, iii, pp. 5 *et seq.*)

89

Association drawn up twenty years later by Marx, "is the great end to which every political movement is subordinated as a means."[1]

The theoretical programme of the youthful Marx, to "seek for the anatomy of civil society in Political Economy," does not, however, mean a simple acceptance of the accomplished results of the preceding period of economic science. Political Economy was, historically, the new science of the bourgeoisie, brought forth by the rising industrial class in its revolutionary fight against feudalism. Now, in a new historical epoch, that revolutionary struggle has come to an end. The bourgeois class rules, both politically and economically, in present-day society. Thus, Political Economy, dealing with the material foundation of the existing bourgeois State, is for the proletariat first and foremost an enemy country. Nor does it lose this character by the fact that parts of the ground held by its outposts are being occupied by the theoretical vanguard of the proletariat. The first task for the representatives of the new revolutionary class in this field is, therefore, to reconnoitre the enemy's position.

In striking contrast to the illusions cherished by many socialists in their time and up to the present day, Marx and Engels never accepted the idea that this same economic science which the proletarian class inherited from the bourgeoisie, could now, by a mere elimination of its inherent bourgeois bias and a consistent working out of its own premises, be transformed into a theoretical weapon for the proletarian revolution. Wherever such an opinion was expressed by the first socialist Ricardians of 1820-30, by the Owenists, or by Proudhon, Rodbertus, and Lassalle, they declared it an "economically false theory," an idealistic application of morality to economics and in its practical consequence a reactionary *Utopia*.[2] They pointed out that

---

[1] See *Address and Provisional Rules of the Working Men's International Association*, printed at the Beehive Newspaper Office, London, 1864.

[2] See Engels, *Preface* to German ed. of *La Misère de la Philosophie*, 1884, pp. VI, ff., and Marx, *Theories of Surplus Value*, III, Pt. 3.

the equality-idea resulting from the epoch of bourgeois "commodity-production" and expressed in the economic "law of value" is still bourgeois in its character. It is therefore only ideologically incompatible with the exploitation of the working class through capital, but not in actual practice. The socialist Ricardians imagined that they could attack the economists on their own ground and with their own weapons. On the basis of the *economic* principle that "it is Labour alone which bestows value," they wanted to transform all men into actual workers exchanging equal quantities of labour. To one of the best of them, Bray, Marx replied that "ce rapport égalitaire, cet idéal correctif qu'il voudrait appliquer au monde, n'est lui-même que le reflet du monde actuel, et qu'il est par conséquent totalément impossible de reconstituer la société sur une base qui n'en est qu'une ombre embellie. A mesure que l'ombre redevient corps, on s'aperçoit que ce corps, loin d'en être la transfiguration rêvée, est le corps actuel de la société."[1] Instead of deriving the demands of socialism and communism, in an idealistic and Utopian manner, from the laws of bourgeois economics, Marx and Engels formulated the materialistic conclusion that "according to the laws of bourgeois economics, the larger part of the product does *not* belong to the workers who have produced it."[2] In order to obviate this state of affairs one must not apply a different interpretation to bourgeois economics but rather, through a real change in society, bring about a practical situation in which those economic laws will cease to hold good and thus the science of economics will become void of contents and ultimately vanish altogether.

Political Economy then, according to Marx, is a bourgeois science. This applies even to Marx's own contributions to the further development of its main doctrines. Marx fought to the end against the mistaken idea that his economic analysis of

[1] See *Misère de la Philosophie*, 1847 (MEGA, I, vi, p. 157).
[2] See Engels, *Preface* to German edition of *La Misère de la Philosophie*, 1884.

KARL MARX

Value applied to any other than bourgeois conditions.[1] Even
the Marxian doctrine of *Value and Surplus Value* is only the final
outgrowth of a conceptual process which, in content, had been
almost completed by the classical bourgeois economists.[2]
Friedrich Engels, immediately after Marx's death, made it quite
clear,[3] and the posthumous publications from Marx's papers[4]
exhaustively proved, that Marx at no time in his life counte-
nanced the opinion that the new contents of his socialist and
communist theory could be derived, as a mere logical consequence, from the utterly bourgeois theories of Quesnay, Smith,
and Ricardo.

How then are we to understand the leading part which, in
spite of all this, Political Economy played in the genesis of Marx's
theory of society, and maintained through all its subsequent
developments ? This in itself shows again the superiority of the
materialistic standpoint. Marx kept aloof from that superficiality
by which many revolutionary theorists in his time and to-day
imagined that by a mere theoretical effort, wishful thinking,
or a simple "change of heart" they could ignore such objective
facts as those investigated by economic science—the very funda-
mentals of all existing social relations. The modern working
class in its independent social movement inevitably starts from
the historical results of the bourgeois revolutionary movement.
At the same time this bourgeoisie and the new mode of production it brought forth, its State and all its other institutions
and ideas, are the very antagonist from whom the proletariat

---

[1] See among other references: *Misère de la Philosophie*, 1847 (MEGA, I,
vi, pp. 149-157); *Critique of Political Economy*, 1859; and Marx's notebook *Oekonomisches en général*, X, 1881-82, from which parts were
published by the Marx-Engels-Lenin Institute as an *Appendix to Capital*,
I, Berlin and Vienna, 1932, pp. 841 ff.
[2] See *Capital*, III, ii, p. 366. See further, Marx's letters to Engels of
24.8.67, and 8.1.68 (MEGA, III, iii, p. 410; and III, iv, p. 6).
[3] See *Prefaces* to German edition of *La Misère de le Philosophie*, 1884; and
to the second vol. of *Capital*, 1885.
[4] See the 3 volumes of *Theories of Surplus Value*, edited by Kautsky from
the unpublished MSS of Marx's *Critique of Political Economy*, 1904-10.

must completely separate its own action and whom it must ultimately conquer in a decisive battle. So must the proletariat, in evolving its own revolutionary thought, start from the results achieved by bourgeois economic investigation. It cannot skip over, in its own materialistic theory, the definite forms of economic science existing historically in the present epoch any more than it can neglect, in its revolutionary practice, the existence of the modern capitalistic mode of production. Only by means of a practical and theoretical action persistently continued for a considerable time through several intermediate phases, can the proletariat carry through the necessary change in the existing conditions of material production and thereby ultimately surpass the social forms of consciousness which are at present bound up with those conditions.

Long before he applied this consequence of his materialistic principle to economic science, Marx had applied it to philosophical thought in the battles waged in the forties between the various groups of young Hegelians, on the question of the impact of "philosophy" (i.e., Hegelian philosophy) on the imminent political revolution. He had opposed the attitude of the philosophical party which derived the revolution immediately from the principles of philosophy just as much as he had opposed that of the anti-philosophical party which turned its back on philosophy. Just as he had done in his previous criticism of philosophy, so now in his criticism of Political Economy, Marx seemed to call out to the socialistic Ricardians, etc., who wished to derive socialism from bourgeois economics : "*You cannot realize Political Economy* (in practice) *without doing away with it* (by theoretical action) ;" and to the "pure" historians, "pure" sociologists, "pure" revolutionary activists, who ignored all economics, "*You cannot do away with Political Economy* (by practical action) *without realizing it* (in theory)."[1]

---

[1] See Marx, *Introduction to a Critique of Hegel's Philosophy of Law* (MEGA, I, I, i, p. 613), and the author's *Marxism and Philosophy*, second edition, 1930, p. 93.

CHAPTER II

FROM POLITICAL ECONOMY TO "ECONOMICS"

CLASSICAL Political Economy, as distinct from the adulterations of the "vulgar" economists of the 19th century and from the more recent attempts at an entirely new start, originated historically as an integral part of the *new science of civil society*, created by the bourgeoisie in its revolutionary struggle to establish this very society. It formed a realistic complement to the great philosophical, political, juridical, moral, æsthetic, and psychological upheaval, through which during the period of the so-called "Enlightenment" the ideological representatives of the rising bourgeois class first expressed the new bourgeois consciousness which corresponded to the change in the real conditions. Even in its purely theoretical form, the new science of Political Economy during this early period, as well as in the first great systems of the Physiocrats, was bound up with the whole of the new bourgeois social science in a natural and ingenuous unity.[1] It is true that Adam Smith separated his economic *Inquiry into the Nature and Causes of the Wealth of Nations* from the "general principles of law and government, and of the different revolutions they have undergone in the different ages and periods of society," as discussed in his academical lectures,[2] just as he had already split another part from that bulky whole in his earlier *Theory of Moral Sentiments*. Yet in his economic work he embraced once more, along with the fundamental economic relations, the whole of the new political and social conditions arising from the development of industry, exchange of commodities, and the division of labour within the new bourgeois

[1] See, e.g., Quesnay, *Le droit naturel* (Daire, Paris, 1846), summed up from this point of view by Marx in Notes of 1845-46 (MEGA, I, vi, pp. 612-13).

[2] See *Editor's Introduction* to E. Cannan's edition of Smith's *Wealth of Nations*, London, 1904.

order of society. Even in the work of Ricardo, in which the classical epoch of Political Economy reaches its close, this "organic" connection between Political Economy and the whole of society is preserved. At the same time, it can be said that the system of Ricardo which, as a true "anatomy" of civil society, formally restricts itself to an ingenious dissection of the material foundations—the skeleton, as it were, of the social body—shows the first symptoms of an impending disintegration. Still more does the subsequent theoretical development of bourgeois economics reveal the inevitable results of the change which during the ensuing period was to strip the bourgeois "production-relations" more and more of their original positive functions as incomparable stimulators and encouragers of the productive forces inherent in the new, industrial society.

This historical process, through which the hitherto progressive forms of the bourgeois production-relations were finally transformed into so many fetters, has since, in spite of temporary interruptions, asserted itself with ever increasing strength. It finds its economic expression in those periodically recurring dislocations of all existing proportions of capitalist production which, since their earliest characteristic occurrence in the first modern economic crisis of the year 1825, have assumed ever greater dimensions and ever more acute forms during the whole of the following century, challenging at their culminating points the whole existence of bourgeois society. There is no need to deal in this connection with the manner in which the curve of "social unrest" during the last hundred years continuously reflected the course of economic development, if not exactly at each point yet in its entire movement. The only point to be discussed here is the difference which prevails between the repercussions on the labour movement of the periodic business cycle, and those more permanent alterations within the whole economic system of modern society which have been described by recent explorers as a "structural change." While the recurring phases of the "normal" industrial cycle are followed by corresponding ups-and-downs in class warfare, there is no such "cyclical" rhythm discoverable in the underlying secular movement. In spite of the intervening longer periods of an apparently undisturbed upswing and prosperity brought about by the temporary defeats, iron-handed oppression, and effective crushing of all existing workers' organizations, the proletarian struggle against the existing capitalist order of society has grown from its first elementary beginnings to embrace ever greater numbers, and to assume ever more efficient, more conscious, and more threatening forms. It has become a veritable war between the oppressing and the oppressed classes, a war conducted on many fronts simultaneously, which sometimes breaks out in open revolts. The first World War, 1914-18, and the first wave of the proletarian world revolution released by the war, challenged the very premises on which during the "restful" intervals of this restless development, the bourgeois economists, and in their wake the moderate socialists, had based their "historical refutation of the Marxian prognoses." The first shock was followed by even stronger charges. The protracted economic crisis and the new series of wars and civil wars terminating the short-lived momentous upswing which had resulted during the 20's from the first apparent recovery of post-war capitalist equilibrum, reflected once more the utter absence of cohesive forces within the present economic system, and finally refuted the illusions by which the economic optimists had conjured up for themselves a complete abolition of crises in "organized capitalism," and of all class oppositions and class struggles in the *"democratic"* or, more recently, in the *"totalitarian State."* Even such things as *machinery* and *money*, formerly so undoubtedly good and useful, have been robbed of their virtue as forces productive of social wealth and turned into forces destructive of social existence. The political and intellectual superstructure of society follows the change in its material conditions. The democratic forms of the State, the liberal ideas of the ascending phase of capitalist commodity production, have everywhere begun to totter. One after another of the safety-valves of the economic and political system is suspended. Emergency and martial law are the rule of common law. War and civil war on a world-wide scale have become the "normal" form of existence of present-day society.

A minor consequence of this universal destruction of the positive social function of bourgeois production-relations manifests itself in the gradual decay of the encyclopædic spirit which had been so conspicuous during that earlier period when Political Economy embraced the whole of the social progress of the community. It is only from a formal point of view that Ricardo's economic system can be regarded as an advance on that of Adam Smith. While Smith had worked out his ideas on an epic scale and, little troubled by logical contradictions, developed the subject matter of Political Economy to a vast totality, Ricardo logically subordinated the whole of the bourgeois system to a unique principle, tracing back all its economic laws to the definition of value in terms of labour time. The theoretical satisfaction offered in Ricardo's *Principles* (and more especially in its first two chapters which, as demonstrated by Marx, virtually contain the whole book) by their originality, unity of the basic view, simplicity, concentration, profundity, novelty, and pithiness,[1] is purchased at the expense of a loss of substance foreshadowing an impending emaciation. The generality aimed at by Ricardo is only the generality of scientific form ; there is nowhere in his work, as there had been in that of Smith, the urge of a wider political aim. Its historical function consisted in summing up the great positive achievements of the classical period of bourgeois economic science and in the formal conclusion of an actually completed epoch.

While thus in Ricardo the turn to formalism was historically necessary and, thereby, theoretically justified, the progressive

[1] See *Theories of Surplus Value*, II, p. 8.

formalistic anæmia of the later period brought none of the great theoretical advantages of which the sceptics and the cynics of present-day "pure" Economics are so proud. They are so convinced of their superiority over the "unscientific" methods applied by the classical economists that they even accept without demur the reproach that their new theoretical science has become a mere plaything, purged of any political significance and of any possibility of application. Following the example of some modern mathematicians, logicians, and physicists, but without in any other respect keeping pace with the achievements of those real sciences, they want to carry on, in a field which cannot otherwise boast of any particular purity, the business of "pure" science, not for any useful purpose but merely "for the greater glory of God."

The actual outcome of this later development of Political Economy was a gradual decay. At the same rate as under the impact of the changed conditions of bourgeois production, bourgeois economic theory abandoned its original comprehensive social tendency, it abandoned also its formal scientific qualities, its impartiality, its logic, and fecundity. "From the year 1830 dates the finally decisive crisis."[1] Henceforth any genuine development of Political Economy was precluded by the real historic development of bourgeois society.

Marxism restored, consciously and on a higher level, the connection between Political Economy and social science which had spontaneously and unconsciously evolved with the bourgeois classicists at an earlier stage. Only for this reason had the science of Political Economy any interest, only thus did it assume its important place in the whole of the Marxian social research. For this reason alone, it appears absurd that so many people should rack their brains to find out why Marx never paid the slightest attention to that "new departure" which, since the middle of the 19th century, is assumed to have been made by an

[1] See *Postscript*, 1873.

altogether new economic science based on subjective value and the theory of so-called "marginal" utility. Marx did take cognizance of every new word, true or false, which was contributed to any economic question during his lifetime, even by the least important Epigone of classical Political Economy. His adherence to the classicists did not make him neglect the work of another school which, to a certain extent, preceded the theorists of "marginal value" in an attempt to reconstruct economic research by stressing "subjective" value (value in use) rather than classical "objective" value (value in exchange). He did not shrink, though he sighed under the burden, from the task of refuting the many inconsistencies of the leaders of the so-called "kathedersozialistische" school, from Rodbertus to Adolf Wagner. His apparent neglect of the new questions raised by the theorists of marginal utility sprang from an entirely different source. By the very principle of his *socio-economic research*, Marx was not interested in the thoughts of people who, though still calling their science "Economics," did not have anything in common with that research into the material foundations of society which had formed the theme of classical Political Economy, any more than he would have been interested in some other auxiliary inquiry into a group of natural and technical facts not particularly important for the historical change of society. An economic doctrine indifferent to its social implications aroused the attention of Marx only when in spite of its purely "theoretical" concern, it afterwards did serve to draw practical application from its purely theoretical contents, and thus, like Duehring's "socialist" doctrine in the 70's, found supporters within the ranks of the workers' movement. This, however, did not take place with the theory of marginal utility until some years after Marx's death when, in Engels' phrase, G. B. Shaw and his followers endeavoured to base a plausible kind of "vulgar" socialism upon "Jevons' and Menger's use-value and marginal-utility theory," in order "to build on this rock the Fabian church of the future." That is why Marx in all his comprehensive criticism of traditional economic theories, never considered the theory of marginal utility while, on the other hand, Friedrich Engels, when editing the third volume of *Capital*, bestowed a critical after-thought upon this newest theoretical attempt, if only in that somewhat curt and deprecatory remark.[1]

[1] See Engels' *Preface to Capital*, III, 1894.

CHAPTER III

A S the revolutionary bourgeoisie had enlightened itself as to the principles of the new industrial society in the new science of *Political Economy*, so did the proletarian class assert its revolutionary aims in the *Critique of Political Economy*. This is not a critique of single results of bourgeois economics from within. It is, fundamentally, a critique of the very premises of Political Economy based upon the new standpoint of a social class which, theoretically as well as practically, goes beyond bourgeois economy. It investigates the tendencies inherent in capitalist commodity production which in the course of their further development produce the necessary basis for the economic, political, and ideological struggle of the proletarian class, and which will ultimately overthrow the bourgeois mode of production and advance to the higher production-relations of a socialistic and communistic society.

The Marxian "critique" is not the first appearance of a genuine principle of criticism as a driving force in the development of economic science. Already in the earlier phases of Political Economy the Mercantile system had been criticised by the Physiocrats, the Physiocrats by Adam Smith, and Adam Smith by Ricardo. Nor was that earlier economic criticism a matter of pure theory. Each new phase of the theoretical development implied a new phase in the real historical development of the capitalistic mode of production. There was no clear distinction ; in fact, every historical phase was in itself a criticism of the preceding phase. For all that, the actual historical and theoretical "subject" of economic science remained unchanged through all these stages. The bourgeois class in its revolutionary struggle against the obsolete forms of feudal production, could not, and did not, distinguish its particular interests as a class from its general interest in the whole of historical progress. Even after the defeat of feudalism, it could still for a considerable time quite honestly regard itself as promoting the general welfare of society. During this phase Political Economy was even striving to co-operate, with the utmost impartiality, in the solution of the new economic problems emerging from the increasingly un-satisfactory conditions of the real people, that is, the actually working section of the as yet undivided industrial society.

That state of things was profoundly changed by the new historical development which set in with the economic crisis of 1825 and with the great political changes of 1830. Henceforward, the new conditions established within bourgeois society no longer permitted an impartial analysis of the economic principles under-lying those conditions. A strictly scientific investigation of social development was possible only from the standpoint of that class whose task in history is to transcend the narrow bour-geois horizon and, ultimately, to do away with classes alto-gether.[1]

The theoretical system of Ricardo marks the turning point.

The complete impartiality of the genuine scientific investigator which appears everywhere in the work of Ricardo, had seemed miraculous already to his contemporaries. "Mr. Ricardo seemed to have dropped from another planet," said Lord Brougham. With faultless clarity, this English banker of the beginning of the 19th century, who nowhere goes beyond the boundaries of the bourgeoisie,[2] presented in his system the inherent disharmonies as well as the harmonious and progressive features of the bourgeois mode of production ; more particularly he revealed the inevit-able opposition arising between the two industrial classes. He

[1] See Marx, *Postscript*, 1873.
[2] "The 'parallelograms of Mr. Owen' appear to be the only form of society which he knew outside the bourgeois one" (Marx, *Critique of Political Economy*).

declared from the outset that the principal problem in Political
Economy is to state the proportions in which the whole produce
of society is allotted to each of the three social classes : the pro-
prietors of land, the owners of capital, and the property-less
labourers.[1] Thus "the contrast of class interests, of wages and
profits, of profit and rent," became indeed, as was later stated
by Marx, the very "pivot" of Ricardo's economic investigation.[2]
    The position of Ricardo in the history of economic science
is precisely analogous to that occupied by Hegel in philosophical
thought, just as in a preceding phase the economics of Adam
Smith had corresponded to the philosophy of Kant. This
analagous historical position appears most clearly in Ricardo's
important contribution to what we have described in an earlier
chapter as the "bourgeois self-criticism."[3] The scientific criticism
of the existing capitalistic system, which pervades the economic
system of Ricardo, surpasses the occasional comments of the
earlier economists on the unpleasant sides of the new bourgeois
conditions even more than the earlier philosophical critics had
been surpassed by Hegel. While in dealing with Hegel we had
to disregard the mystifying form of his statements in order to
find out his realistic advance on his predecessors, the superiority
of Ricardo's criticism over that of his forerunners is clear like
day. His critical statements not only surpass all previous criticism
in their sweeping power of generalization and in the irresistible logic of their reasoning. A more decisive difference appears
in their very premises, namely, in the fact that they rest no
longer on that naive faith in the fundamental perfection or the
unlimited perfectibility of the new world order, which had
prevailed among the economists of the preceding period quite
as much as among the philosophers.
    Political Economy in its first period had been optimistic and

---

[1] See Preface to first edition of Ricardo's *Principles of Political Economy
and Taxation*, 1817.
[2] See *Postscript*, 1873; see also Marx's letter to Weydemeyer, 5.3.52.
[3] See above, pp. 61 *et seq.*

confident to the extent that along with the blessings of the new bourgeois mode of production it could afford to acknowledge their purchase price. "Not for a single moment did it deceive itself as to the birth pains of wealth, but what is the use of crying over historical necessity?"[1] Even for Adam Smith it had still been fairly easy, in his great inquiry into the best possible ways to raise the general wealth of society, to regard the interests of the "inferior order" of the wage-labourers as well as those of the two "superior orders" (profit and rent). He had even endeavoured to oppose the tendency of the newly arrived bourgeoisie to monopolize for itself the advantages won in a common battle and to bring definitely to the front the neglected interests of the common man. He did not thereby endanger, but rather tightened the apparent unity of the two industrial classes which were at that time still busy conquering the last surviving prerogatives of the landed aristocracy. A different situation was faced by Ricardo when in a supplementary chapter added to the third edition of his *Principles* he did not uphold the favourable view on the effects of machinery which he had expressed in the preceding chapters of his work but which in the meantime had been proved to him by Sismondi to be erroneous both in fact and in theory. While he had then emphasized the "general good" which must of necessity be brought about by "these mute agents which are always the produce of much less labour than that which they displace,"[2] he now carefully re-examined his earlier position. A more realistic consideration of the "influence of machinery on the interests of the different classes of society" led him to the conclusion that

the opinion entertained by the labouring class, that the employment of machinery is frequently detrimental to their interests, is not founded on prejudice and error, but is conformable to the correct principles of Political Economy.[3]

[1] See *Capital*, I, p. 558.
[2] See *Principles of Political Economy*, chap. i, § 5.
[3] *Ibid.* chap. xxxi.

No wonder that the later pseudo-scientific apologists of capitalism should denounce him on this count as the Father of Communism. Said a leading American economist in 1848 :

> The system of Mr. Ricardo is one of discord . . . it tends to foster enmity between classes and nations . . . His book is the right textbook for the demagogue who aims at power through agrarianism, war, and plunder.[1]

All post-Ricardian developments of Political Economy testify to the fact that the historical struggle waged between the progressive industrial class and the obstructive forces of feudal oppression had now been finally superseded by a new revolutionary conflict arising within bourgeois society between the two hitherto united classes produced by modern industry itself —bourgeoisie and proletariat.

The first of the various schools to work out the scientific results of classical Political Economy under the changed historical conditions of the 19th century sprang up immediately after Ricardo's death. From this school started the attempt with which we have dealt above, to use the Ricardian theory as a weapon against the existing economic system of society and thus to derive anti-bourgeois conclusions from bourgeois principles.[2] But in the main the spokesmen of this new school contented themselves with celebrating the victory of the Ricardian principles over all pre-Ricardian economics in a series of splendid tournaments which were for the most part displayed in scattered review-articles, occasional papers, and pamphlets and were, after long oblivion, rediscovered and recognized in their historical importance, mainly by the endeavours of Marx.[3] This last polemical intermezzo preceding

[1] See H. Carey, *The Past, the Present, and the Future*, Philadelphia, 1848. See also the belated abuse of "Ricardo, Jew and Marxist" by the German Minister of Propaganda, Goebbels, at the Congress of the National Socialist Party in Nuremberg, 1936.
[2] See above, p. 90 *et seq.*
[3] See the detailed discussion of this whole school in *Theories of Surplus Value*, III.

105

the final collapse of the fighting spirit in bourgeois economic theory—a skirmish resembling, as Marx said, the "Sturm und Drang" period of economic science that had raged in France after Dr. Quesnay's death, but not more than "Indian summer reminds us of the spring"[1]—covered roughly the decade 1820 to 1830. After that it dragged on in ever weaker manifestations to the Repeal of the Corn Laws in England in 1846 and to the outbreak of a new revolution on the continent in 1848-49.

Another tendency of post-Ricardian economics is represented by a school of pseudo-scientific writers who flattened, diluted, and gradually entirely dispersed the theoretical results reaped from the work of classical economists. The theoretical contents of the prolific writings of this school are most aptly, if somewhat cruelly, described by Marx as a mere "vulgarization" of the scientific achievements of Political Economy. The "vulgar" successors of the great classical economists have, indeed, not added any new contribution to that genuine work of discovery by which their scientific predecessors had discerned the inner relations of the modern bourgeois mode of production and thus brought forward the necessary premises for its genetic presentation. Scientific analysis was everywhere replaced by mere conceptual reflection. That simple reproduction of the given external conditions, which for the classicists had been merely one of the constituents of their theory—its "vulgar" element—was now finally set up as a separate existence. Yet this was not the lowest point reached in the gradual decay of a formerly vigorous and vital science. A still more complete loss of scientific character was seen, when later, along with the further development of the real oppositions inherent in the life of bourgeois society, economic science itself split in mutually opposing parts. Bourgeois economists, when no longer confronted with their own internal dissensions, but with a group of socialistic dissenters opposing them from without, promptly threw over all

[1] See *Postscript*, 1873.

semblance of unbiassed theoretical research. From a mere neglect of the progressive tasks of true science, they turned to a conscious defence of existing bourgeois conditions against the impending socialistic menace embodied in the writings of Sismondi, Owen, Fourier, St. Simon. The more the stern outlines of the class strife asserted themselves in the actual development of capitalist society, the more the economists applied themselves to a misrepresentation and, ultimately, to an entire negation of these new historical tendencies. At each further step in the unavoidable development of "class" and "class discord" within reality, they strengthened their desperate efforts to keep these embarrassing topics entirely out of their theoretical picture. They even endeavoured to purge the classical concepts of any such impurities wherever they had already been introduced into economic theory by their great scientific predecessors. Thus bourgeois economists became even incapable of a faithful registration of external facts. By the combined effect of all these self-established obstructions, the "vulgarized" economic theory of the 19th century became poorer and poorer in theoretical content. There is, however, a difference between the earlier stage when, for instance, Say had "vulgarized" Adam Smith, and the later stage when MacCulloch, Bastiat, and others "vulgarized" Ricardo. In the earlier phase the "vulgarizers" had found their material as yet unfinished, and thus had been compelled to contribute, though in a diminishing degree, to the solving of real economic problems. In the later phase they dropped all independent theoretical effort and occupied themselves with a mere plagiarizing of the doctrines of Ricardo and with an arguing away of their unpleasant aspects.[1]

The deductions which the socialist Ricardians had been unable to draw, and which the "vulgar" economists had deliberately dodged, were formulated fifty years later by a new school of

[1] See Marx, *Theories of Surplus Value*, III, pp. 281 *et seq.*

economic research. The true conclusions of classical Political Economy were drawn by Marx. The "critical" tradition of the classical epoch of Political Economy was revived by the Marxian "Critique" of Political Economy in *Capital*. This new criticism, however, was more than a transition from a given phase to a further developed phase of economic science. It implied a change of the class which henceforth was to be the historical as well as the theoretical "subject" of all Political Economy. While previous criticisms had for their practical aim a further "development" of the bourgeois mode of production, the Marxian criticism aims at its complete overthrow.[1] "Critique" of Political Economy, then, is the theory of an impending revolution.

Not only Marx and Engels, but all revolutionary Hegelians of the 40's and 50's of the last century, had used the word "critique" in this large historical sense.[2] The terminology fell into complete oblivion during the sad period of decline which set in after the collapse of the Chartist movement and the

[1] For a most succinct statement of the matter discussed in this Chapter see Rosa Luxemburg in *Neue Zeit*, XVIII, ii, p. 182: "Classical Political Economy, with invincible logic, finally resulted everywhere in a form of self-criticism, namely, the criticism of the bourgeois order. Ricardo, in England, provided the direct starting-point for a whole school of English socialists (Thompson, Gray, Bray, and others); in France, the first "flattener" of the classical economists, Say, was immediately followed by Sismondi; in Germany, we find socialist sympathies already in Rau, who was followed by Rodbertus and Thuenen. Marx completed the transformation of Political Economy into its opposite, a socialist analysis of capitalism."

[2] See the writings of Ruge, Bruno Bauer, Feuerbach and other left Hegelians which already use the term "critique" generally in their titles, one improving upon the other in ever new variations. From among the earlier writings of Marx and Engels we note: Marx, *"Critique" of Hegel's Philosophy of Law*, Engels, *Outlines of a "Critique" of National Economy* (both in the first and only volume of the *German-French Yearbooks*, published by Ruge and Marx, Paris, 1844); *Towards a "Critique" of National Economy* (Marxian MSS. of 1844, now published MEGA, I, iii, pp. 31 *et seq.*); *The Holy Family*: *"Critique" of the Critical Critique"* (pamphlet against Bruno Bauer and his followers by Engels and Marx, Frankfurt, 1845); *The German Ideology*: *a "Critique" of the New German Philosophy as represented by Feuerbach, B. Bauer, and Stirner, and of German Socialism and its various Prophets"* (MSS. by Marx and Engels, 1845-46, now published MEGA, I, v).

triumph of the counter-revolution in the whole of Europe consequent upon the defeat of the Paris proletariat in June, 1848. Thus a complete abandonment of all revolutionary "critical" tendencies in theory coincided with the abandonment of the last residues of a practical revolutionary tendency. Marx and Engels were the only ones who rescued from oblivion both the practical and the theoretical aspects of a truly revolutionary "critique."[1]

[1] See Marx—*Critique of Political Economy*, 1859, and *Capital, a Critique of Political Economy*, 1867.

CHAPTER IV

SCIENTIFIC VERSUS PHILOSOPHICAL CRITICISM OF POLITICAL ECONOMY

MARX'S approach to Political Economy was from the outset that of a critical and revolutionary student of society rather than that of an economist. Yet a long period was still required before, from the first discovery of Political Economy as an "anatomy of civil society" through a series of intermediate phases, he arrived at his final scientific and materialistic investigation and critique of the whole complex of ideas and facts constituting the historical existence of "Political Economy."

Marx was already an outspoken revolutionary and even a proletarian socialist at the time when he regarded a really developed "Political Economy" as it existed in England and France as being in itself revolutionary progress, and practically identified the aims of Political Economy with the aims of socialism. He contrasted this modern form of relating industry to the State, or the "world of wealth" to the "world of politics," with the reactionary form in which that "main problem of modern times" had then begun to occupy the attention of the Germans. "While the problem in France and England is worded Political Economy, or wealth controlled by society, in Germany it is termed, National Economy, or nationality controlled by private property."[1] If we apply to Marx the terms which he, but a short time later, was to apply to a similar standpoint, we may say that during this short first period Marx had criticized politics only from the standpoint of economics, but had not yet extended his revolutionary criticism to the economic basis

[1] See Marx, *Introduction to a Critique of the Hegelian Philosophy of Law*, 1844 (MEGA, I, 1, i, p. 612). For an early anticipation of the later critical standpoint, see Friedrich Engels, *Outlines of a Critique of National Economy*, 1844 (MEGA, I, ii, pp. 377-404).

itself; or that up to now he had merely "criticized Political Economy from the standpoint of Political Economy."

By the time when he had raised this objection to his first socialist antagonist, Proudhon, Marx himself had adopted an altogether different standpoint which utterly transcended all economic science in an apparently final manner. His *economico-philosophical manuscripts* dating from this second period,[1] and the economic fragments inserted in a mainly philosophical work written at the same time,[2] anticipated all the critical and revolutionary conclusions which were later embodied in *Capital*. Yet this new critical insight was couched in a highly philosophical language and appeared much more as a materialistic continuation of the old philosophical struggles among the different Hegelian schools than as a scientific criticism of the contents and premises of Political Economy. Instead of dealing directly with the theories and concepts of the great classical economists, Marx dealt rather with the idealistic, that is, insufficient reconstruction and criticism which these concepts had in the meantime found in the philosophy of Hegel and of the right and left Hegelians of the 1830's and 40's. For example, he disposed of the socio-economic phenomenon which he was later to solve in a rational way in his critical exposure of the "Fetishism of Commodities," by a reference to the then most fashionable Hegelian term of "human self-alienation." He summed up his criticism of Proudhon in the sentence: "Proudhon conquers economic alienation only within the bounds of economic alienation."[3] In the same manner his criticism of other fundamental economic phenomena started from the assumption that "Hegel takes the position of modern Political Economy"[4] and that, therefore, a materialistic exposure of the idealistic shortcomings of Hegel's

---

[1] See MEGA, I, iii, pp. 33-172.
[2] See Marx and Engels, *The Holy Family*, 1845 (now reprinted MEGA, I, iii, pp. 173-388).
[3] *Ibid*, p. 213.
[4] *Ibid*, p. 157.

philosophical criticism of the economic terms is equivalent to a final refutation of Political Economy itself.

Marx began to free himself from the remaining vestiges of his former philosophical creed by a comprehensive criticism of all post-Hegelian philosophy. In this he was joined by Engels. As a first result of their life-long co-operation, which after some more or less frustrated earlier attempts was now really beginning, Marx and Engels during the next two years worked out in detail the contrast prevailing between their own materialistic and scientific views and the various ideological standpoints represented by their former friends among the left Hegelians (Feuerbach, Bruno Bauer, Stirner) and by the philosophical belles-lettres of the "German" or "true" socialists.[1] Thus, they finally broke with what Marx later called their "former philosophical conscience."[2] From this thoroughly changed standpoint Marx now cruelly criticized the somewhat bewildering manner in which his former philosophical criticism of Political Economy in the meantime had been further worked out by Proudhon.[3] He showed that Proudhon did not treat the economic categories as theoretical expressions of historical conditions, corresponding to a definite stage in the development of material production, but as "pre-existing eternal ideas," and thus ultimately fell back on the standpoint of bourgeois economics.[4] Such criticism of Proudhon's philosophical mystification of economic concepts was undoubtedly justified. But Marx's new anti-philosophical tendency was now so strong that, instead of supplanting Proudhon's bad philosophy by a better and more scientific criticism of Political Economy, he rather confronted Proudhon's un-

[1] See MEGA, I, v, pp. 1-544.
[2] See *Preface* 1859.
[3] See *Misère de la philosophie. Réponse à la philosophie de la misère de M. Proudhon*, 1847, Chapter II, *La Métaphysique de L'economie politique* (MEGA, I, vi, pp. 175-228); see further the letter dealing with the same question written by Marx to Annenkov, 28.12.46, printed in *Mouvement socialiste*, vol. XXXIII, Nos. 249-50, pp. 141 *et seq.*)
[4] See Marx's letter to the editor of the *Sozialdemokrat*, 24.1.65 (printed in Nos. 16-18, 1865).

scientific criticism with the science of Political Economy itself, i.e., with Ricardo's theory of value.[1] Thus he no longer reproached Proudhon for not having passed critically beyond the narrow bounds of economic science. He now reproached him for sharing, as an economist, the "illusions of speculative philosophy" and for not yet having entered the realm of a really scientific Political Economy.

Only with the next stage of this long and somewhat circuitous development do we reach the period, during which Marx finally worked out his own *critical economic theory* which is, at the same time, the basic part of his materialistic theory of the historical development of society and of the proletarian revolution. The first mature fruit of this new stage is contained in the masterly lectures which Marx delivered to the German Workers' Educational Association at Brussels in 1847 and later published, in a revised form, in his own revolutionary paper during the 1848 revolution.[2] Outline and contents reveal that we have here the first fragmentary statement of that comprehensive exposition of the "economic conditions underlying all present-day class wars and national struggles," which, later, after being further worked out and many times entirely recast was to appear as *Das Kapital*.[3] The most conspicuous difference is that Marx in the earlier work does not yet start from the analysis of "commodities" in general but from a particular kind of commodity —*wage-labour*, and from the opposition between the two main classes of modern capitalistic society which directly springs from the appearance of that commodity. We find, moreover, in this

[1] See note by Rjasanov to the German translation of Marx's letter to Annenkov in *Neue Zeit*, XXXI, p. 822.
[2] See *Neue Rheinische Zeitung*, 5.4.-ii.4.1849 (now reprinted MEGA, I, vi, pp. 473-99).
[3] See the *Leading Article* of *Neue Rheinische Zeitung*, 4.4.49, in which Marx outlined the topics to be discussed in the subsequent articles and thus, at the same time, the general scope of his planned economic work. This article was added as a general introduction to the pamphlet, in which Engels re-edited the Marxian articles under the title *Wage-Labor and Capital*, 1891.

first scientific exposition the striking description (pivotal for all subsequent developments and unsurpassed, in trenchant power, even by Marx's own later formulæ) of "capital" itself, which is defined as not being a relation between *men and nature*, but as *a relation between man and men based on a relation between man and nature*—a specific historic form of a social relation arising and decaying with the rise and decay of modern industrial or "capitalistic society."[1]

The working out of this first scientific exposition of Marx's revolutionary criticism of Political Economy was interrupted by the outbreak of the February Revolution,[2] just as in a later period of world history, Lenin's presentation of "The Marxian Doctrine of the State and the Task of the Proletariat in the Revolution" was interrupted by a situation calling for the performance of that very task.[3]

After the final defeat of the abortive European revolution of 1848-49, Marx made the most of the long years of involuntary leisure which were forced upon him as an exile in London, by making "an entirely fresh start" in his economic studies.[4] The ultimate form of his materialistic theory, which resulted from that new and prolonged period of economic and social research, is at the same time Political Economy and a criticism of Political Economy. It works out the classical system of bourgeois economy and ultimately transcends all phases and forms of bourgeois economy. It shows the most general ideas and principles of Political Economy to be mere fetishes disguising actual social relations, prevailing between individuals and classes within a definite historical epoch of the socio-economic formation.

---

[1] See MEGA, I, vi, pp. 482 *et seq.*
[2] See *Preface* 1859.
[3] See Lenin, *Postscript* to *State and Revolution*, 1917, with the concluding remark equally characteristic of both authors—that "it is more agreeable and useful to experience the revolution than to write about it."
[4] See *Preface* 1859.

CHAPTER V

THERE appears in the successive phases of Marx's theory,
besides the main line of a continuous growth of the critical
revolutionary standpoint, another line of development which,
to a certain extent, runs contrary to the first. Hand in hand with
increasing stress on a strictly materialistic and scientific approach,
goes a greater emphasis on economic theory itself, as against
a mere critical attack on its philosophical, historical, and practical premises. It seems as if Marx during the further study of the
vast unexhausted material accumulated during the classical
epoch of Political Economy that he found heaped up in the
vaults of the British Museum, was more and more strongly
impressed by the lasting significance which the scientific results
of classical Political Economy were bound to have for the new
revolutionary class, for a really materialistic theory of bourgeois
society, and for a practicable way to its revolutionary overthrow. Just as the tremendous depression and stagnation following the defeat of the Paris workers in 1848 had imposed upon
the materialistic investigator a long period of leisure for his
ever-expanding, ever-deepening economic studies,[1] so at the
same time many revolutionary impulses within the actual
workers' movement were forcibly repressed in their genuine
practical function. A new stage of development seemed to be
opened for Capitalism with the discoveries of gold in California
and Australia—discoveries which attracted the most active
members of the working class and thus further paralyzed even the
faintest attempts at recovery within the European revolutionary

[1] See the reminiscence of this quiet period, during which the echo of the
Taiping revolt and the new spiritualistic fad of table-tipping provided the
only diversion, in a footnote to *Capital* : "One will remember how China
and the tables began to dance when the rest of the world appeared to
stand still *pour encourager les autres.*"

115

movement. All those historical changes were reflected in the later development of Marx's revolutionary theory. The social revolution of the proletariat was now mainly represented as a necessary development of society, during which capitalistic production by the working of an unevitable economic law brings forth its negation with the inexorability of a natural process.[1] He did not for this reason, commit himself to the so-called fatalist tendency "discovered" over and over again in some of Marx's phrases by the later bourgeois critics and by their supporters within the labour movement. A closer investigation reveals that even in that gloomiest period, both of the proletarian movement[2] and of his own career, Marx kept himself far away from any fatalism. Still, it is a definitely changed pattern of revolutionary action which was henceforward sketched out by the materialistic theory for the historical movement of the workers' class. The question as to whether that change resulted in a strengthening or a weakening of the revolutionary movement can only be answered by taking into account the historical circumstances prevailing at the time, or rather, through the entire historical period. We merely note that the new phase of Marx's revolutionary science and the increased importance which was now assigned to economic theory within its frame,[3] arose from a particular historical situation and suggested a form of behaviour adapted to that particular situation. Marx's materialistic theory, grounded on firm economic foundations, seemed to point out a new way to the workers, who had now passed the period of their first Utopian enthusiasm and spontaneous aggressive activity. Though this new way might not

[1] See the sub-section on the "Historical Tendency of Capitalist Accumulation" in *Capital*, I, xxiv.

[2] See the impressive description of these conditions in the *Inaugural Address* of the *Working Men's International Association*, 1864.,

[3] See the interesting remark made by Engels in his review of Marx's book, *Critique of Political Economy*, in the London emigrants' newspaper, *Das Volk*, No. 14, of 6.8.1859: "The whole theoretical existence of the German proletarian party emanated from the study of Political Economy. . . ."

ensure a quick and easy advance to victory, nor even a direct approach to decisive battles, yet in comparison with the meagre chances of the earlier period, it afforded a distinctly better opportunity, nay even a practical certainty of success.

This element of disillusionment and dearly-bought sobriety which is inherent in the later phases of Marx's "materialism" and is largely responsible for the tremendous effect which Marxism was to exert upon the workers' movement during the ensuing historical period, was produced by the historical conditions of the 50's. It is, at the same time, both historically and theoretically connected with another and much more general chain of historical events. The proletarian revolution of the 19th century, which so far had found its most powerful and most conspicuous theoretical expression in the revolutionary materialism of Marx, appears, under a secular aspect, as being itself a mere *second phase* within the whole of the modern revolutionary movement.[1] Thus it shares, to a certain extent, that more general "disenchantment" which after the conclusion of the great French Revolution was first proclaimed by the early French theorists of the counter-revolution and by the German Romanticists. This idea of disenchantment has, in fact, exerted a considerable influence upon Marx mainly through Hegel, and has thus directly entered into the "materialistic" Marxian theory of the modern workers' movement. Nay, more, we may go still further back and find within the materialistic theory of the proletarian revolution some traces of the revolutionary tradition of the Jacobinic Convention of 1792-94. This particular phase of the French revolution which was afterwards exalted over and over again by Marx, Engels, and Lenin as a model of the highest political sagacity and energy, had, likewise, been a "second" and sobered phase in contrast to the first exuberant and illusionary phase of 1789-92.

---

[1] See the first paragraphs of Marx's pamphlet, *The 18th Brumaire of Louis Bonaparte*, published in *Die Revolution*, New York, 1852.

On all these grounds the Marxian materialistic and economic theory bears the specific characteristics of a *theory of the second phase of the proletarian revolution*, and has actually made its first entrance in all countries where it became the dominant revolutionary theory at the very time when an analagous historical situation had arisen in that particular country. Even in *Russia*, where revolutionary Marxism was to make world history by a first great victory of its principle,similar historical circumstances accompanied its reception. The revolutionary social democratic, i.e., "Marxist," principle was inaugurated in Russia since 1883, according to the testimony of the best authority on the subject,[1] mainly by a pamphlet of Plechanov which, under the heading *Socialism and Political Struggle*, endeavoured to "open up a new way for the *defeated* revolutionary movement through which it could secure for its cause *a certain, if not immediate, victory.*" Instead of following by a conscious and violent action the model set by the preceding generation of Russian revolutionaries, it was to rely on the socio-economic process of development which would "slowly but unavoidably undermine the old régime" and through which the Russian working class "in an historical development proceeding just as inexorably as the development of capitalism itself," would finally "deal the death blow to Russian absolutism" and would then "join, as an equal member, the ranks of the international proletarian army."[2]

In a similar way, Marx and Engels themselves upon several occasions expressed the idea that the different degrees of "maturity," or the preparedness of the workers' movement in various capitalistic countries to accept the Marxian materialistic theory, more or less depended upon the experience gained by each section of the workers concerned during a preceding phase of Utopian illusions and immediate revolutionary attempts.

[1] See the statement made by Rjasanov in his *Preface* to the German edition of Plechanov's book on *Fundamental Problems of Marxism*, 1929.
[2] See Plechanov's pamphlet of 1883, as quoted in the text, and similar remarks in the works of all later Russian Marxists.

This assumption of two definite phases, one "Utopian," the other "scientific," through which every modern labour movement must pass in its historical development, was finally stated by Friedrich Engels in his well-known pamphlet on *The development of Socialism from a Utopia to a Science*. Since its first appearance in France, in 1880, this pamphlet was spread under this and under various other titles in large editions throughout the world and became as significant for the various *Social-Democratic Movements* preceding the World War, as have been, for other historical phases of the modern workers' movement, *The Communist Manifesto* of 1848, Marx's *Address and Rules of the Working Men's International Association* of 1864, and Lenin's pamphlet on *State and Revolution* of 1917.

Whatever the reasons, there is no doubt that Marx, during his later development, linked himself more and more closely with the scientific results of classical Political Economy. The Marxian "Critique" as contained in the second and third books of *Capital* (which after his death were edited by Engels), and even in the first book edited by Marx himself, not infrequently gives the unwary reader the impression of being no longer directed against the whole of the preceding bourgeois economic science, but only against those superficial and apologetical forms into which the truly scientific statements and concepts of the great classical thinkers had degenerated with the post-classical or "vulgar" economists. Yet this is by no means the real significance of Marx's economic and social theory. It is easy to clear up some ambiguous statements[1] by reference to those sections of the first Chapter of *Capital* in which Marx stated with the utmost precision the difference between his critical economic theory and the doctrines presented by even the greatest and most advanced thinkers of the classical epoch of bourgeois Political Economy.[2]

[1] See, e.g., *Capital*, III, ii, p. 366, and *Theories on Surplus Value*, III, pp. 71-72.
[2] See *Capital*, I, pp. 46 *et seq*, footnotes 31-33.

CHAPTER VI

ECONOMIC THEORY OF CAPITAL

IN our presentation of the economic theory of Capital, we shall confine ourselves to one or two results of the Marxian teaching, extremely abstract in appearance, which include, in our opinion, the revolutionary kernel of the Marxian theory and thus constitute its fundamental and epoch-making importance. It is this, in fact, which explains why the teaching of Marx has gained and retained, for almost a century, the active support of millions of revolutionary workers in all parts of the world, and which even to-day forces from the most bitter opponents of the proletarian class movement an unwilling tribute, in that they announce as the aim of their reactionary and counter-revolutionary endeavours—*War against Marxism.*

Marx himself, in a letter which he wrote to Engels soon after the appearance of *Capital,* designated as the "three fundamentally new elements" of his book, the following :

(1) that in contrast to *all* earlier economics which from the outset had dealt with the detached fragments of surplus value in their fixed forms of Rent, Profit, Interest, as given entities, he first treated the general form of Surplus Value, in which all those elements are still comprehended in an undivided unity like the uncrystallized components in a chemical solution ;

(2) that, without exception, economists had missed the simple fact that if a commodity is the sum of the "value in use" and the "value in exchange," the labour entailed in the production of the commodity must possess the same two-fold character, while the mere analysis for "labour sans phrase," as in Smith, Ricardo, etc., must inevitably stumble upon something inexplicable. *This is indeed the whole secret of the critical conception ;*

(3) that for the first time wages are shown to be an irrational manifestation of some other relation hidden behind them.[1]

All these innovations are of decisive importance with regard to the ultimate aim of the Marxist theory, the critical transformation of economics into a direct historical and social science dealing with the development of material production and of the class struggle. That goal, however, is not reached by an immediate disintegration of economics as a particular form of knowledge but by a further theoretical development which brings into relief the inherent contradiction between the economic categories and principles and the actual facts which had hitherto been presented in their guise. While Marx seems merely to proceed with the work begun by the great bourgeois economists, his further development of their theories is guided in every case by a definite critical purpose. A more refined, more comprehensive, more thorough, and more consistent analysis serves to advance the traditional economic concepts and theorems to that point where the practical reality behind them, i.e., their historical and social contents become tangible and subject to a critical attack.

Thus the Marxian definition of value in terms of labour differs from the classical definition not by its conceptual form but rather by a closer connection with the underlying social conditions. Similarly, the advance made by the famous Marxian doctrine of surplus value, as stated by Marx himself, is new only because of the more comprehensive synthesis, by which he reduced to a common denominator the various phenomena of profit, interest, and rent as described by the classical economists. Nor does the new Marxian definition of wages, not as the "price of labour" but as the price of labour-power, amount to a major scientific discovery since the best classical writers, and, indeed, Marx himself in his earlier period had already applied the former

[1] See Marx's letter to Engels of 8.1.1868 (MEGA, III, iv, p. 6).

term in exactly the same sense which was later more fully expressed by the more elaborate description.[1] Both these apparent technicalities and, in fact, the whole of the Marxian improvements upon classical economic theory are important, not for their purely formal advance over the classical concepts, but for their definite transfer of economic thought from the field of the exchange of commodities and of the legal and moral conceptions of "right" and "wrong" originating therein to the field of material production taken in its full social significance. For example, the economic concept of a *surplus value* existing in the form of goods and money and competed for by its rival claimants is now transformed into the concept of a *surplus labour* performed by the real workers in the workshop under the social domination exerted upon them by the capitalist owner of the workshop. Furthermore, the "free labour contract" of the modern wage labourer is, by an apparent change of terminology only, now revealed as a real sale of the labour-power of the wage-labourer to the capitalist in return for wages, and thus as a social oppression and exploitation of the labouring class persisting within an assumedly "free" and democratically ruled society.

Marx begins the further theoretical development of the economic categories at the point where classical political economists had ended, i.e., with an analysis of "value" based on the distinction of a "value in use" and "value in exchange," and with the reduction of "value" to "labour." These two scientific discoveries of the last stage of bourgeois classical economics, of which, as they were then represented, the one was bound to remain entirely sterile, and the other led only to a one-sided

[1] See Marx, *Wage Labour and Capital*, 1848 (MEGA, I, vi, pp. 473 *et seq.*) The full equivalence of the terms used by Marx in his earlier and later period is clearly demonstrated by the fact that Engels in his later editions was able to substitute the new term "price of labour power" in all cases where Marx had originally used the term "price of labour" without any change of the real argument.

and formalistic further development, were used by Marx to work out his new concept of *"commodity-producing labour"* which was henceforth to serve as a pivot for a new understanding of the whole conceptual system of Political Economy.

The distinction between use-value and exchange-value, in the abstract form in which it had been made by the bourgeois economists, (and had, in fact, already been applied by Aristotle to the commodity production of Antique Society) did not provide any useful starting-point for a materialistic investigation of bourgeois commodity production as a particular social form. It was insufficient also for theoretical reasons. The concept of use value was only perfunctorily mentioned by them as a presupposition of exchange value, and exchange value alone was treated as a real economic category.[1]

With Marx, as we have seen in a former chapter, use value is not defined as a use value in general, but as the *use value of a commodity*. This use value inherent in the commodities produced in modern capitalistic society is, however, not merely an extra-economic presupposition of their "value." It is an element of the value, and itself is an economic category. The mere fact that a thing has utility for any human being, say for its producer, does not yet give us the economic definition of use value. Not until the thing has social utility (i.e., utility "for other persons") does the economic definition of use value apply.[2]

Just as the use value of the commodity is economically defined as a *"social use value"* (use value "for others"), so is the

---

[1] See the first three paragraphs of Ricardo's *Principles*; the first introduces the distinction between use value and exchange value by way of a quotation from Smith; the second emphasizes use value as an absolutely essential presupposition of exchange value; while in the third it is definitely dismissed from all further investigation.

[2] See *Capital*, I, p. 7. See further, for the most detailed presentation of Marx's view on this question, his polemics against Rodbertus and Adolf Wagner in the *MSS.* of 1881-82 grouped under the heading *Oekonomisches en général* (*X*) in Marx's papers (published as an Appendix to the Marx-Engels-Lenin Institute's edition of *Capital*, 1932, pp. 841 *et seq*, particularly pp. 846-53). This was Marx's last word on economics.

123

specifically useful labour which goes into the production of this commodity defined economically as a *"social labour"* (labour "for others"). Thus, Marx's *"commodity-producing labour"* appears as a social labour in a two-fold sense.[1] It has, in common with labour in other stages of the historical development of production, the *general social character* of being a "specifically useful labour," which goes to the production of a definite kind of social use value. It has, on the other hand, the *specific historical character* of being a "generally social labour," which goes to the production of a definite quantity of exchange value. The capacity of social labour to produce definite things useful to human beings (a general condition of the Circulation of Matter going on between Man and Nature) appears in the *use value* of its product. Its capacity for the production of a value and a surplus value for the capitalist (a particular characteristic of labour which derives from the particular form of the social organization of the labour process under the conditions of the capitalistic mode of production within the present historical epoch) appears in the *exchange value* of its product. The fusion of the two social characteristics of commodity-producing labour appears in the "value form" of the product of labour, or the *"form of commodity."*

Only thus critically modified, is the *theory of labour value* a suitable starting-point for an economic theory in which labour is considered not merely formally and in one of its aspects but in its full material realization. The earlier bourgeois economists when speaking of labour as a source of wealth, had likewise thought of "labour" in terms of the various forms of real work, though they did so only for the reason that their economic categories were as yet undeveloped, and still in the process of separation from their original material contents, vague and indeterminate. Thus, the Mercantilists, the Physiocrats, etc., successfully declared the true source of wealth to lie in the labour

[1] See *Capital*, I, i, § 2, *The Two-fold Character of Commodity-producing labour.*

expended in the export industries, trade and shipping, in agricultural labour, etc. Even with Adam Smith, who from the different branches of labour definitely advanced to the general form of commodity-producing labour, we find that concrete aspect retained, along with the new and more formalistic definition which is also expressed in his system and was later to become the exclusive definition of value in the work of Ricardo, and by which labour is defined as an abstract and merely quantitative entity. This same abstract form of labour, which he correctly defined as exchange-value producing labour, he at the same time, irrationally enough, declared to be the only source not only of value (exchange value) but also of the material wealth of the community, or use value.

This doctrine which still obstinately persists in "vulgar" socialism, and which is unjustly imputed to scientific socialism by its bourgeois critics, is according to Marx economically false. In so far as "labour" is regarded in its specific character as useful labour, and, in the same way, "wealth" in its material form as an object of utility, labour is *not* the only source of wealth. (If this were so, it would be difficult to explain why in present-day capitalistic society just those persons are poor who hitherto have had that unique source of all wealth at their exclusive disposal, and even more difficult to account for the fact that they remain unemployed and poor, instead of producing wealth by their labour). But it is just here, in the very inconsistency of his economic theory, that a remembrance of the concrete reality of human labour lingers in the mind of Adam Smith. In praising the creative power of "labour" he was not thinking so much of the forced labour of the modern wage-labourer, which appears in the value of the commodities and produces capitalistic profit, as of the general natural necessity of human labour, which produces things useful and beautiful. Likewise, his naive glorification of the "division of labour" achieved in these "great manufactures," by which he understood the whole of modern capitalist production, does not so much refer to the extremely imperfect form of present-day capitalistic division of labour (arising through commodity production and exchange) as to the general form of human labour vaguely fused with it in his theoretical exposition.[1] "Adam Smith's contradictions," said Marx later, "are significant in so far as they contain problems which he indeed does not solve, but which he reveals just by contradicting himself."[2]

In the further development from Smith to Ricardo, Political Economy becomes more consistent—and one-sided. Even now, bourgeois economists do not deny that there are two characters inherent in the commodity, use value and exchange value. But they deal only with "value of exchange" as the true economic value. While immersed in their "economic" definition of "value" in terms of labour, they appear to have quite lost sight of the other aspect of labour which had, at least unconsciously, been taken into consideration by the older economists, that is, of labour as a specifically useful activity, which brings forth as its product a definitely useful object (a use value). "Political Economy," said Marx, "nowhere explicitly and consciously distinguishes between labour represented in value and the same labour so far as it is represented in the use value of its product."[3]

Marx has reintroduced in a new form real, concrete labour into Political Economy. He deals with "labour" not in the indefinite, ambiguous, and vacillating form as it had appeared in the writings of the older bourgeois economists ; not as the labour of the commodity-producer, or as the materially and formally free labour of the independent master craftsman, who had control over his own material means of production, and

[1] See *Misère de la Philosophie*, II, § 2 (MEGA, I, vi, pp. 193 *et seq.*), and *Capital*, I, xii, sects. 4-5, particularly footnotes 57 and 70, and the passages there quoted from Smith's and Ferguson's works.
[2] See *Theories of Surplus Value*, I, p. 171.
[3] See *Capital*, pp. 46-47, footnote 31.

ECONOMIC THEORY OF CAPITAL

who exchanged the product of his labour in the form of a commodity for another kind of commodity, or the product of
another form of an equally free and independent labour. Marx
deals with labour in its present unambiguous, and definite, form
of *labour producing a commodity for another person*, i.e., of labour
formally paid to its full value but actually exploited ; formally
free, actually enslaved ; formally the independent labour of an
isolated worker, actually collective labour performed by proletarian wage-labourers who are separated from the material
means of production and to whom their own tools and the *social
character of their own labour*,—that is, the productive power of
what would be under otherwise similar conditions the produce
of an isolated worker, now increased a thousandfold by the
social division of labour—stand opposed in the form of *capital*.[1]
Political Economy is now no longer a science of commodities,
and a science of labour only indirectly, and in an abstract and
one-sided manner. It becomes a direct science of social labour,
of the productive forces of that labour, of their development and
afterwards their enslavement by the fixed forms of the production-relations prevailing in present-day bourgeois society and,
finally, of the emancipation of the productive forces inherent in
present society by the revolutionary action of the proletarian
class. A glance at the first volume of Marx's *Capital* will suffice
to convince us of the completely changed character of this
science of economics.

From the very beginning the meticulous analysis of the most
general economic categories ("Commodity," "Money," and
"Transformation of Money into Capital") in the first chapters
of Marx's work, adheres only in appearance to "that turbulent
sphere of the exchange of commodities which is taking place
on the surface of commodity-producing society, open and
visible to all." In truth, from the opening sentence to the final
conclusion, the Marxian analysis serves to make us look through

[1] See *Theories of Surplus Value*, III, p. 308.

those higly abstract and sophisticated categories of the bourgeois economists, to disclose their "fetish character," and to demonstrate the specific social character of bourgeois commodity production lying behind them. It becomes highly transparent while dealing, in its later parts, with the sale and purchase of a commodity of a very special composition, labour-power. It finally passes from the realm of commodity-exchange into another sphere entirely, the "hidden haunts of production, on whose threshold we are faced with the inscription : No admittance except on business."[1] From now on the *labour process*, or what is according to Marx but another name for the same thing, the *process of material production*, both in its material and historical aspects, constitutes the subject matter of the economic theory of *Capital*. That applies not only to chapters 5, 8, 11, 12, 13, etc., which are especially devoted to the analysis of labour and, which, quantitatively, make up half of the first volume but, as revealed by a closer examination, to the whole book.[2] Just as *Leviathan* is but the nominal title of Hobbes's political work, so *Capital* is only nominally the subject of Marx's new economic theory. Its real theme is *labour* both in its present-day economic form of subjugation by capital and in its development, through the revolutionary struggle of the proletariat, to a new directly social and socialist condition.

[1] See *Theories of Surplus Value*, III, pp. 177-78.
[2] See *Capital*, III, ii, pp. 366-67.

CHAPTER VII

THE FETISHISM OF COMMODITIES

POLITICAL Economy, which considered bourgeois commodity production as the final achievement, valid for all time, of a rational and natural system of economic order, had reduced all economic concepts to *value*, and all economic laws to the *law of value*. It had defined the exchange value of commodities which appears in the purchase and sale of the products of labour as a given *"quantity of value,"* independent of the particular kind of utility or *"use value"* of the several commodities, and dependent only on the labour-time expended on their production. Notwithstanding an often conflicting outside appearance it adhered to the essential truth of this definition.

Bourgeois economics did not, however, get beyond that formal concept. Even the best and most consistent among its exponents who were fully aware of its objective economic contents and had not mistaken "value" for an arbitrary term (as superficial thinkers had done even then), had taken the circumstance that relative quantities of labour are represented in the value-relations of its products, and thus labour in value, as an evident fact not requiring any further investigation.

A further generalization of the categories which had been regarded by bourgeois economists as the ultimate generalization of their science became possible only when the narrow horizon of bourgeois economic science was left behind by a new scientific advance, which was based on the changed view-point of the revolutionary proletarian class. According to Marx, the most general category within the realm of economics is no longer "value" or the "quantity of value," but the *value form of the product of labour* or the *form of commodity* itself.

Even this fundamental form of the bourgeois mode of production is a "general form" only from the standpoint of a merely

129

"economic" science (and it represents, indeed, an extreme limit of the generalization which is possible from that restricted standpoint). It is at the same time, from the more advanced viewpoint of the Marxian Critique of Political Economy, on the contrary, a *specific mark* by which the bourgeois mode of production is distinguished from other historical forms as a particular form of social production. The transition from the one concept to the other, which is implied in the whole of Marx's economic work, is explicitly made in that final paragraph of the first chapter of the first volume of *Capital*, so important for the stand taken by Marx against all bourgeois economics, which bears the rather mysterious title of *The Fetish-character of the Commodity and its Secret.*[1]

[1] See *Capital*, I, i, sect. 4.—The final standpoint of Marx in this matter is only imperfectly expressed in the other two passages which might be referred to in the existing text of *Capital* (III, xlviii) and in the *Theories of Surplus Value* (III, 7, sub-section 1, under the heading "The Capital Fetish"). It is best here, as in many other cases, to take only the first volume of *Capital*, which was prepared for press by Marx himself and, in addition, the second volume, as edited from later Marxian MSS. by Engels, as an absolutely authentic presentation of the Marxian standpoint. The other works which figure as the continuation of *Capital* (i.e., the 3rd. vol. edited by Engels, and the *Theories of Surplus Value* edited by Kautsky) should be regarded only as what they actually are, viz., older presentations of the Marxian thought which in no case can be taken to supersede the statements contained in vols. 1 and 2 and, in fact, are all drawn from *earlier* MSS. Moreover, these older MSS. used by Engels and Kautsky, being first drafts and preliminary notes, often do not contain those important statements showing the practical impact of the preceding theoretical analyses, which Marx used to reserve for the final revision. (See Engels' communications in the *Preface* to *Capital*, III, pp. ix-x). A careful distinction between the earlier and later, the final and preliminary statements of Marx has a particular importance for the subject under discussion, as just here the further development of the Marxian thought has continuously remained in a state of flux. Thus, in the *Critique of Political Economy* of 1859, the first chapter on "Commodity," which presents the earliest version of the later first chapter of *Capital*, was only in the last moment added to the rough draft, which, instead, had only contained a section on "Value." (See MEGA, III, ii, pp. 349 and 308-12). Again, the sparse references in the "*Critique*" of 1859, to the "mystification of the commodity," which appears in the "exchange value," were only in the last revision of the text of *Capital* enlarged to form the independent examination of *The Fetish character of the Commodity and its Secret*, which now forms the concluding section of the first chapter of the first volume of *Capital*.

The "fetish-character" of the commodity, reduced to its simplest form, consists in the fact that man's handiwork assumes a peculiar quality which influences in a fundamental way the actual behaviour of the persons concerned. It does not wield that remarkable power (as the earlier economists had believed) by an eternal law of nature, yet it is endowed with such power under the particular social conditions prevailing in the present epoch of society. Whence arises this mysterious character of external things which is described by political economists as their "value," and which attaches itself to the products of labour as soon as they are no longer produced directly for use but for sale as "commodities?" The value of a commodity does not arise either from its physical qualities or from its specific utility, nor even from any specific qualities belonging to the labour involved in its production. The value relations appearing in the exchange of the products of labour as "commodities" are essentially not relations between things, but merely an imaginary expression of an underlying social relation between the human beings who co-operate in their production. Bourgeois society is just that particular form of the social life of man in which the most basic relations established between human beings in the social production of their lives become known to them only after the event, and even then only in the reversed form of relations between things. By depending in their conscious actions upon such imaginary concepts, the members of modern "civilized" society are really, like the savage by his fetish, controlled by the work of their hands. *Commodities* and, in a still more conspicuous form, the particular kind of commodity which serves as a general medium of exchange, namely, *money*, and all further forms of capitalistic commodity production derived from those basic forms, such as capital, wage-labour, etc., are examples of that fetish form assumed by the social production-relations of the present epoch. What Marx here terms the *Fetishism of the World of Commodities* is only a scientific expression for the same thing that he had described earlier, in his Hegel-Feuerbach period, as "human self-alienation"[1] and which had, indeed, formed the real foundation for this particular calamity which befalls the Hegelian "idea" at a definite stage of its speculative development.[2]

Marx had, however, emphasized as early as this, the real economic and social facts underlying that Hegelian philosophical term. Much more clearly than Feuerbach and the other philosophizing Hegelians he had recognized that the various forms in which that philosophical category enters into present-day society—as "property, capital, money, wage-labour, etc.", are by no means a kind of self-created "idealistic figment of our imagination." On the contrary, all those "alienated forms" actually exist in present society as "very practical, very material

[1] See above pp. 111 et seq. The first definite application of the philosophical concept of "alienation" to the economic concepts of money, value, credit, etc., was made by Marx in his unpublished *Notes of 1844*, on reading a work of the elder Mill (MEGA, I, iii, pp. 531 et seq.), and in the *Economico-Philosophical Papers* written in the same period (*ibid*, p. 29 et seq. esp. pp. 81 et seq.). Among the most striking statements in those early papers we find the far-reaching discovery that the estrangement, the alienation of the labourer, does not only arise from his relationship to the products of his labour, but exists also within the productive activity itself (pp. 85 et seq.). On the other hand, Marx was already fully aware of the fact that even such apparently higher developed forms of capitalist organization as the credit and bank systems, which the followers of St. Simon and other Utopian socialists had idealized as being "a gradual undoing of man's separation from matter, of capital from work, of private property from money, of money from man," amount in truth to an even more infamous and extreme self-alienation in that their element is no longer a commodity, metal, paper, etc., but indeed is the very moral existence, the social existence, the inmost heart of man himself; in the disguise of trust and confidence of man to man—the highest degree of distrust and a "complete estrangement" (pp. 533-35). About the same time Marx noted for future use an interesting term employed by the Utopian Socialist Pecqueur—of the *vertu magique* of fertility which is conveyed to the dead element of matter by labour, that is, by the living man. That early reference to the particular form which the general fetishism attached to all commodities assumes in the particular commodity, called "labour power," is the first indication of the specific connection between what Marx later called the "fetish character of the commodity' and his doctrine of "surplus value."

[2] See Hegel *Phenomenology of the Mind* (Works, II, 1932, p. 594) and its critical analysis by Marx (MEGA, I, iii, pp. 153-72).

things."[1] For example, the fact that one of the worst cases of that "self-alienation of humanity" appears in present-day bourgeois society as the contrast of the *haves* and the *have-nots* is by no means the outcome of a mere conceptual or spiritual process. "*Not having* is the most desperate *spiritualism*, an entire negation of the reality of the human being, a very positive *having*, a having of hunger, of cold, of sickness, of crimes, of debasement, of imbecility, of all forms of inhumanity and abnormality."[2] And in striking contrast to the "idealistic" dialectics of Hegel who had endeavoured to annihilate the existing self-alienation of man in society merely by an imaginary philosophical annihilation of the objective form, in which it is reflected within the human mind,[3] Marx denounced the utter insufficiency of a mere effort of thought to handle the real forms of that self-alienation which exist in the present-day bourgeois order of society and of which the "alienated" concepts of the bourgeois economists are only an outward expression. It is, for this purpose, above all necessary to abolish, by the practical effort of a social act, its underlying real conditions.[4] Marx had also called by name the social force which was to perform that revolutionary action : "the communist workers in the workshops of Manchester and Lyons" and the "associations" founded by them.[5]

The later Marxian criticism of the "fetish-character" inherent in the commodity "labour-power" and, indeed, in all "economic" categories differs from that earlier criticism of the economic "self-alienation" mainly by its scientific and no more philosophical form.

[1] See Marx, *The Holy Family* (MEGA, I, iii, p. 224).
[2] *Ibid*, p. 212.
[3] See MEGA, I, iii, pp. 156 *et seq.*, esp. p. 162.
[4] The 1844 writings of Marx quoted in this chapter anticipate, with regard to the economic use of the term "self-alienation," that more general criticism which Marx and Engels two years later in their critical exposure of "*The German Ideology*" directed against every conceivable application of the term.
[5] See MEGA, I, iii, pp. 211 *et seq.*, 222 *et seq.*

Modern capitalistic production both historically and theoretically rests on the separation of the real producers from their material means of production. Thus it is but a juridical illusion that the workers either as individuals or as members of an amalgamated group of labour-power owners freely dispose of their property. The common assumptions underlying the "fetishistic" concept of an individual, and even of a collective, "bargaining" with regard to the commodity "labour power" are still derived entirely from the dreamland of the free and equal individuals united within a self-governed society. The propertyless wage labourers selling through a "free labour contract," their individual labour powers for a certain time to a capitalistic *"entrepreneur"* are, as a class, from the outset and for ever a common property of the possessing class which alone has the real means of labour at its disposal.

It is, therefore, only one part of the truth that was revealed by Marx in the *Communist Manifesto* when he said that the bourgeoisie had "resolved personal worth into exchange value," and thus replaced the veiled forms of exploitation applied by the "pious, chivalrous, ecstatic, and sentimental middle ages" by an altogether *unveiled exploitation.*[1] The bourgeoisie replaced an exploitation embroidered with religious and political illusions by a new and more refined system of concealed exploitation. Whereas, in mediæval society even the utterly material tasks of production were performed under the spiritual disguise of "faith" and of an "allegiance" due by the "servant" to his "master," in the new era of "Free Trade," conversely, the continuing exploitation and oppression of the labourers is hidden under the pretext of the "economic necessities of production."[2] The scientific method of concealing this state of affairs is called *Political Economy.*

From the critical exposure of the fetishism inherent in the commodity "labour-power" there was but one step to the dis-

[1] See *Communist Manifesto* (MEGA, I, vi, p. 528).
[2] See *Capital*, I, pp. 680-682 and III, ii, p. 367.

covery of the most general form of the "economic" delusion appearing in the "commodity" itself. Just as the classical economists had derived all other terms of their science from the "value" appearing in the exchange of commodities, so Marx now traced back the delusive character of all other economic categories to the fetish-character of the "commodity." Though even now that most obvious and direct form of the "self-alienation of the human being" which occurs in the relation between wage-labour and capital, keeps its decisive importance for the practical attack on the existing order of society, the fetishism of the *commodity labour-power* is at this stage for theoretical purposes regarded as a mere derivative form of the more general fetishism which is contained in *commodity* itself.

Thus the Marxian criticism of the existing order is transformed from a particular attack on the class character into a universal attack on the fundamental deficiency of the capitalistic mode of production and the structure of society based upon it. By revealing *all* economic categories to be mere fragments of one great fetish did Marx ultimately transcend all preceding forms and phases of economic and social theory. Political Economy itself had in its later development rectified such primitive misconceptions as that by which the adherents of the so-called "monetary system" had regarded *money*, in the form of gold and silver, as a product of nature, endowed with some peculiar social qualities, or the physiocratic illusion that *rent* grows out of the earth, not out of society. It had at its highest point of development theoretically interpreted "*interest*" and "*rent*" as mere fractions of the industrial "*profit*."[1] However, even the most advanced classical economists remained under the spell of that same fetish which they had already practically dissolved by their own theoretical analysis, or fell back into it, because they had never succeeded in extending their critical analysis to that general fundamental form which appears in the *value-form* of

[1] See *Capital*, III, ii, p. 366, and *Theories of Surplus Value*, III, pp. 571-72.

the labour products and in the *form of commodity* itself. The great theoretical art of classical Political Economy here met its historical barrier. "The value form of the labour product is the most abstract but also the most general form of the bourgeois mode of production which is thereby historically characterized as a particular kind of social production. By misconceiving it as an eternal and natural form, he will overlook the particular character of the value form and thus also that of the commodity form, which appears further developed as money form, capital form, etc."[1] Marx was the first to represent that fundamental character of the bourgeois mode of production as the particular historical stage of material production, whose characteristic social form is reflected reversedly, in a 'fetishistic" manner, both in the practical concepts of the ordinary man of business and in the scientific reflection of that "normal" bourgeois consciousness —Political Economy. Thus the theoretical exposure of "the fetish character of the commodity and its secret" is not only the kernel of the Marxian *Critique of Political Economy*, but, at the same time the quintessence of the economic theory of *Capital* and the most explicit and most exact definition of the theoretical and historical standpoint of the whole materialistic science of society.

The theoretical disclosure of the fetishistic appearance of commodity production has a tremendous importance for the practical struggle carried on by those who are oppressed in present-day society and who as a class are rebelling against this oppression. In view of the "good intentions" and scrap of paper proclamations constantly repeated by the official spokesmen of present-day economics and politics that *"the worker shall no more be regarded as being a mere article of commerce,"*[2] the very statement

[1] See *Capital*, I, pp. 47-48, footnote 32.
[2] See, e.g., *Versailles Treaty*, article 427, where at the instigation of the American Federation of Labour this principle was formally accepted as the first of the *"Eight principles for the regulation of the conditions of labour"* embodied in the Rules of the then constituted League of Nations.

of the existing fact that under present conditions *the worker is and remains an article of commerce*, becomes an open rebellion against the paramount interest of the ruling class in keeping intact both the fetishistic disguise and the underlying actual conditions. It forcibly re-establishes the responsibility of the ruling bourgeois class for all the waste and hideousness which by the "fetishistic" device of bourgeois economics had been shifted from the realm of human action to the sphere of so-called immutable, nature-ordained relations between things. For this reason alone, any theoretical tendency aiming at an unbiassed criticism of the prevailing economic categories, and the corresponding practical tendency to change the social system of which they are an ideological expression, is opposed from the outset by the overwhelming power of the classes privileged by the present social order and interested in its maintenance. The ultimate destruction of capitalistic commodity-fetishism by a direct social organization of labour, becomes the task of the revolutionary proletarian class struggle. A theoretical expression of this class struggle and, at the same time, one of its tools, is the revolutionary *Critique of Political Economy*.

CHAPTER VIII.

THE "SOCIAL CONTRACT"

MARX'S criticism of the fetish character of commodity production inaugurates a new epoch in the development of social science. First and foremost, the concept of "civil society," that is, of the sum and aggregate of the *material conditions prevailing in the new commodity-producing society*, could not be worked out in its full social significance by the ideological protagonists of the revolutionary bourgeoisie as long as the fundamental economic relations of the new form of society were disguised as mere relations of things. Moreover, the concept of "civil society" which had been initiated at an early time by such forerunners as Ibn Khaldoun, the Arab,[1] in the 14th century and after a temporary eclipse was revived by Vico, the Italian,[2] and the "English and French of the 18th century,"[3] had suffered from a considerable vagueness and ambiguity as to the limits between the newly discovered sphere of "civil society" on the one hand, and the traditional sphere of "political society" or the State on the other hand. While the bourgeois theorists were quite able to distinguish their "civil society" from the old feudal form of the State, they confused and identified it with the new political institutions and ideas of the bourgeois State. Instead of limiting the term of civil society to the basic relations springing immediately from the (old or new) economic conditions,[4] they

[1] See *Prolegomènes historiques d'Ibn Khaldoun*, translated into French by M. D. De Slane, in Notices et Extraits des manuscripts de la bibliotheque impériale, vol. XIX, Paris 1862, p. 86.
[2] See Vico, *Principii di una scienza no uva d'interno alla commune natura delle nazioni*, 1725.
[3] See the Marxian statement quoted above p. 20.
[4] See Marx, *German Ideology* (MEGA, I, v, p. 26): "Civil society as such develops with the bourgeoisie; however, the social organization springing directly from production and commerce which formed in all times the basis of the State and of other phenomena of the idealistic superstructure, has been continually called by the same name."

138

used both terms rather indiscriminately as one comprehensive name for *the whole of the new social relationships* which had now at last been agreed upon by the human individuals through the conclusion of the "social contract," be it that this contract was reached in full harmony and complete freedom (as the more superficial exponents of the new theory had it) or that, after the more realistic concepts of Hobbes, Rousseau, and Hegel, it was forced upon an unwilling opposite party after a mortal struggle according to the right of the strongest.

Marx's materialistic description of the social nature of the relations which are "reversely" expressed in the categories of Political Economy as relations between things, has a similar significance for the proletarian movement of the present epoch as Rousseau's theory of the "social contract" had for the bourgeois revolution of the preceding historical epoch. The unmasking of the fetish character of the commodity contains the rational and empirical solution of a problem which the social theorists of the 18th century had not even set themselves and which such later bourgeois schools as the romanticists, the historical school, the adepts of the "organic" theory of the State, and Hegel had approached in a more or less mystical way. At first sight, there seems to be no great difference between Marx's demonstration of the "secret" contained in the "form of commodity" and the manner in which Hegel had dealt with the apparent mystery of the fact that history, made by men, follows a plan not conceived by men. Just as Hegel said that "in world history out of the actions of men comes something quite different from what they intend and directly know and will ; they realize their interests, but something further is achieved thereby which is internally comprised in it, but of which they were not conscious nor did they aim at it,"[1] so Marx dwells on the contradiction that men in exchanging the products of their labour

[1] See Hegel, *Philosophy of History, General Introduction,* I, ii, under the heading *"Individuality."*

as commodities and in ultimately producing them for no other purpose than that of such exchange, just thereby achieve that qualitative and quantitative social division of labour which afterwards appears to them as an external thing in the definite value-relations of the commodities exchanged or in the value-form of the commodity. "They don't know it, but they do it."[1] He emphasizes the paradox still more by the often repeated statement that the utter absurdity pertaining to the fetish categories of Political Economy is only an unavoidable outward appearance of an equally fundamental absurdity underlying the real capitalist mode of production and that thus, in the economic value-relations of the commodities, the social relations of isolated commodity producers appear to them as "what they really are."[2]

However, all these paradoxes are for Marx, otherwise than for Hegel, only a means by which he compels the reader who is still under the spell of the traditional bourgeois concepts to look at such a palpable and everyday thing as a commodity as containing anything like a "secret" at all. The uncovering of this "secret" is not reached by Hegelian wizardry but by a rational and empirical analysis of a historically existing phenomenon and of the real social facts underlying its appearance. For the prophets of the 18th century, Quesnay, Smith, and Ricardo, the "natural" starting point of all social life was the free *individual* as he just emerged from the feudal bonds of the Middle Ages and from the close connection with physical and geographical conditions by which he had been hampered in the earlier epochs of his development. The new concept of society starts from the specific *social connection* which for the single individual living and acting in this society is given from the outset as a quasi-external fact independent from his knowledge and purpose. From the bourgeois point of view, the individual citizen thinks of the "economic" things and forces as of something entering into his private life from without. He uses them as instruments for his

[1] See *Capital*, I, p. 40. [2] *Ibid*, p. 39.

140

subjective ends and, on the other hand, is restrained by them to a certain extent, in his otherwise free-willed actions. According to the new concept, individual men with all their actions and sufferings move, from the outset, in definite social circumstances arising from a given stage in the development of material production.[1] These social circumstances and their historical developments, though set by human beings themselves in their united action, are nevertheless for the individuals concerned given just as irrevocably and as "objectively", as is, according to Hegel, the philosophical "idea" appearing in history or, according to a still more ancient and respectable theory, God the Almighty appearing in the flesh. Yet they are no longer regarded by Marx as a superhuman authority like the Absolute Reason which, according to Hegel's description, is "as cunning as it is powerful" and which lets men "wear one another out in the pursuit of their own ends" and thus, without direct interference, nevertheless "attains her own purpose only."[2] This concept of Hegel's was, after all, nothing else than an idealization of the bourgeois concept of the benefits derived from free competition. According to Marx's critical principle, the contradiction in question results, on the contrary, from a deficiency in the present capitalistic regulation of social production compared with that higher form which is to-day no more a mere matter of imagination, but an objective historical development and a real goal gradually approached by the workers in their revolutionary class struggle. It is writ large on the face of the formulæ of Political Economy that they "belong to a type of social organization in which the production process controls men, not yet men the production process."[3]

Such high ideals of bourgeois society as that of the free, self-determining individual, freedom and equality of all citizens in the exercise of their political rights, and equality of all in the eyes

[1] This point is best presented by Marx in *Introduction*, 1857, pp. 710 *et seq.*
[2] See Hegel, *Encyclopædia*, § 209.
[3] See *Capital*, I, p 48.

of the law, are now seen to be nothing but *correlative concepts to the Fetishism of the Commodity*, drawn from the existing system of exchange. All these far-flung additions to the basic form of the commodity-fetish which for a time had served as stimulators of material progress are to-day but ideological expressions of a particular type of production-relations that have degenerated into mere fetters of the further development of the productive forces of society. The great illusion of our epoch that capitalistic society is a society consisting of free and self-determining individuals can only be maintained by keeping the people unconscious of the real contents of those basic relations of the existing social order which by the fetishistic device of the economists had been disguised as objective and unchangeable conditions of all social life. Only by representing the real social relations between the classes of the capitalists and the wage labourers as an inevitable result of the free and unhampered "sale" of the commodity "labour power" to the owner of the capital, is it possible in this society to speak of freedom and equality. "The bourgeois law," said Anatole France, "forbids with the same majesty both the rich and the poor to sleep under the bridge."

CHAPTER IX

THE LAW OF VALUE

THE social organization of labour which is hidden under the apparent value relations of commodities, is achieved in the bourgeois mode of production without the will and knowledge of the individual commodity producers. Bourgeois commodity production is, therefore, at the same time a private and a social, a regulated and an unregulated ("anarchic") production. It seems as if by an undisclosed decree of "God" or "Providence," "Fortune" or "Conjunction," it were laid down beforehand what kinds and what quantities of socially useful things should be produced in every branch of production. But the individual capitalist "producer" learns only subsequently—through the saleable or unsaleable quality of his commodity, through the price vacillations of the market, through bankruptcy and crisis —if and how far he has acted in accordance with that unknown rule, the economic "plan" of capitalistic reason. Bourgeois economists have over and over again referred in poetical metaphors to this inscrutable mystery of their own social existence. Just as Adam Smith spoke of an *"invisible hand"* which leads the individual trader to promote an end which was no part of his intention[1] so other economists before and after him referred to the "play of free competition," to the "automatism of the market," or to a "law of value," which would apply to the movements of production and circulation of commodities in the same way as the law of gravity applies to the movements of physical bodies. In fact, the concept of an entirely automatic regulation of the whole industrial production brought about by the mere exchange of commodities among entirely isolated commodity producers on a national and a cosmopolitan scale

[1] See *Wealth of Nations* Book IV, ii.

143

was not more than an *"ideal type"* even in those earlier periods when it first struck the eyes of the bourgeois classical economists. It was never fully realized in actual capitalistic production.

Nevertheless, there is in bourgeois commodity production an unwritten law which rules the production and exchange of labour products as commodities. But this is by no means an unchangeable law of nature ; it is a *"social law"* which resembles a genuine physical law only in its apparent independence from our conscious volition and purpose. Like any other social rule, it holds good only under definite circumstances and for a definite historical period. Marx in dealing with the *"so-called Primitive Accumulation of Capital"* showed what enormous effort was needed to give birth to this fundamental law of the modern bourgeois mode of production and the other "eternal" laws connected with it. He exposed the series of more or less forgotten sanguinary and violent acts by which in real history the actual foundations of those so-called natural laws have been brought into existence. (The expropriation of the workers from their material means of production forms the basis of the whole process.) Marx has likewise shown in detail that even in a completely developed commodity production the law of value does not apply in the sure and efficient manner of a genuine natural law or of a generally accepted Providence, but is realized only by a succession of frictions, vacillations, losses, crises, and breakdowns. He says that "in the haphazard and continually fluctuating relations of exchange between the various products of labour, the labour time socially necessary for their production forcibly asserts itself as a regulating natural law *just as the law of gravity does when the house collapses over our heads.*"[1]

With all these deficiencies, the *law of value* is the only form of social organization of production which exists to-day and is, indeed, the only kind of "social planning" which conforms to the principles of modern competitive or commodity-producing

[1] See *Capital*, I, p. 4.

society. It belongs to the ironical whims of History that just that self-contradictory belief in a "consciously planned commodity production" which lies at the bottom of the first Utopian schemes of a "National Bank", at which "any member of the community might lodge any kind of produce and take out of it an equal value of whatever it may contain,"[1] and which was afterwards voiced in various forms by the successive schools of "social reformers," has been adopted to-day by the official spokesmen of the bourgeois class. But though this illusion is as old as capitalism itself and obstinately persists in spite of theoretical arguments and in spite of the breakdown of all projects brought forward for its realization, it is unsound both from the orthodox principle of bourgeois economic science and from the materialistic viewpoint of Marxism. It is interesting only as an ideological reflex of the deep-rooted contradictions inherent in the very principle of capitalistic commodity production.

Such difference as there is between the earlier epoch when the progressive Free Traders regarded every "interference" of a State—not yet entirely their own—as an oppressive disturbance, and the present phase when even some of the most "orthodox" economists have turned from self-help to State subvention, does in no way indicate a gradual conquest of the animal-like "struggle for existence," prevailing among the isolated commodity producers of early bourgeois society, by the growing collective reason of all capitalists grouped together and organized in the "State" and in the more or less authentic institutions of a so-called "Public Opinion." There is thus only a difference of degree between the more or less numerous "interventions" of the early bourgeois State into the "free play of competition," and the increasingly rapid succession of ever more intrusive measures, by which to-day everywhere in the old and in the "new," in the fascist and in the still democratically governed

[1] See John Gray, The Social System, A Treatise on the Principle of Exchange, 1831 and, for a critical refutation, Marx, Critique of Political Economy, 1859.

145

capitalistic countries, an apparently new attempt is made to "*control*," to "*correct*," or to "*steer*" the existing economic system. Such measures serve at the utmost to weaken temporarily or even merely to disguise some of the most obstructive results of capitalistic production. Instead of ousting the planlessness resulting from the fetish-form of commodity-production, they merely stampede the unique form, in which production had been heretofore "planned" within capitalistic society, and utterly destroy the only "organization of labour" possible under capitalism.

This increasing *destruction* of its own foundations is forced upon present-day capitalism by an objective development of its inherent tendencies. It is produced by the ever-increasing accumulation and concentration of capital ; by the growing monopolist tendencies of the big industrial and financial combines ; by the increasing appeal to the State to rescue "the community at large" from the dangers brought about by the impending collapses of hitherto proud and tax evading private enterprises ; and by the hyper-ultra-super-dreadnought demands for subsidy raised by the various direct and indirect producers of armaments encroaching ever more on the field formerly occupied by the activities of the less directly war-producing industries. In trying to escape from the periodical crises which threaten more and more the existence of bourgeois society, and in a desperate attempt to overcome the existing acute crisis of the whole capitalist system, the bourgeoisie is compelled, by continually fresh and deeper "interferences" with the inner laws of its own mode of production, and continually greater changes in its own social and political organization, to prepare more violent and more universal crises and at the same time, to diminish the means of overcoming future crises. In organizing peace it prepares for war.

The futility of any attempt to deal with "competition's waste" within the existing forms of production and distribution becomes even more evident when we proceed from the elementary form of the "commodity" to the further developed form of "the worker transformed into a commodity," or from the general historical character of bourgeois production to its inherent *class character*.

Just as the Utopian Exchange-Banks, Labour Certificates, and other endeavours to organize commodity production are repeated in the half-hearted "planning schemes" of the frightened economists and "socially minded" big capitalists to-day, so the first unwieldly attempts of the insurrectionary workers of Paris to wrest from the "revolutionary" government of 1848 some form of realization of the workers' "right to work" are echoed in the various measures by which the democratic and fascist countries try to dispose of the increasing menace of *Unemployment* by a more or less compulsory organization of the labour market. And just as in the first case Marxism answered the capitalist "planners" that the only organization of production conformable to commodity production is the law of value, so sober materialistic criticism of the schemes to supplant the glaring insufficiency of the free "labour market" by some form of public regulation must start from the premise that the transformation of the workers into a saleable commodity is but a necessary complement of that other "transformation" on which all modern capitalistic production rests both historically and in its actual existence—the transformation of the workers' tools and products into the non-workers' "capital." In fact, the most "benevolent" attempts to deal with the modern plague of mass unemployment have hitherto invariably led to an utter failure. There is more an apparent than a real progress in the new deals offered to the growing numbers of the unemployed by their capitalistic rulers to-day, as against those now almost forgotten times when the only cure foreseen by the most "philanthropic" spokesmen of the bourgeoisie was the Workhouse. Now as then, the final result of the endeavours to exterminate both the old form in which unemployment periodically recurred in the industrial cycle, and the new "structural," "technological," "chronic" form in which it has come to stay, is one or another disguised form of that compulsory service whose real character is revealed in the Labour Camps and Concentration Camps of National Socialist Germany,"[1] Behind these "normal" remedies offered in times of peace there stands, as ultima ratio, the mass-employment offered by a new war, and already partially anticipated by a hitherto unheard of extension of the direct and indirect armament industries both in the fascist countries and in democratic Britain and pacifistic U.S.A. The best form of "Public Works" under capitalistic conditions, as was most aptly remarked by a critic of Roosevelt's New Deal,[1] is always War itself which over all other measures to "create work" has the incomparable advantage that it will never cause an undesirable glut of the market because it destroys the commodities it produces simultaneously with their production and, incidentally, destroys a considerable portion of the "excessive" workers themselves.[2]

The positive importance of all attempts made on the basis of the existing capitalistic conditions to create a so-called (lucus a non lucendo !) *"organized capitalism"* lies in another field entirely from that presumed by its ideological promoters—the "planning school" of modern capitalistic economics. The feverish endeavours to supplement the defects of "free" capitalistic commodity production confirm the gravity of those defects and thus inadvertently reveal the fettering character of the existing capitalistic production-relations. They put into sharper relief the incongruence between an ever more efficient organization of production within the single workshop or private capitalistic

---

[1] See the remarks of Engels in a letter to Bernstein of 23.5.1884 which appear to-day as a prophetic anticipation of the ultimate capitalistic realization of the "right to work" in Nazi prisons, labour camps, and other forms of unpaid compulsory work.

[2] See Stolberg and Vinton, *Economic Consequences of the New Deal*, 1935.

trust and the "organic disorganization" prevailing throughout capitalistic production. The futile schemes to keep in "normal" proportions the increasing mass of unemployment and pauperism illustrate once more the capitalistic "law of population" first enunciated by Fourier and later scientifically demonstrated by Marx that within the capitalistic system all methods for raising the social productivity of labour coincide with an extension of the relative surplus population, or the industrial reserve army kept at the disposal of capitalistic industry as a potential supply of labour power for the rapid increases of production in times of prosperity and for the full utilization of the existing capacities of production in war.[1]

There is, furthermore, a considerable difference between the same measures when offered by the capitalists in distress and when thrust upon them by the conscious action of the workers themselves. That difference may, at first, not be a difference in the purely economic contents. Yet it is a difference of social significance. "The right to work taken in its bourgeois sense," said Marx with reference to the struggles of the Paris workers in 1848, "is a contradiction in terms, an impotent pious intention ; but behind the right to work there stands the control of capital, and behind the control of capital the appropriation of the means of production by the associated working class, that is, the abolition of wage labour, of capital, and their mutual dependence. Behind the 'right to work' stood the insurrection of June."[2] Finally, a few of the new developments which are to-day featured as achievements of the "planning idea" may serve to work out within the narrow bounds of the capitalistic production-relations some of the formal elements which, after the overthrow of the existing mode of production, will be totally stripped of the residues of their capitalistic origin and thus usefully applied in building up a really co-operative and socialistic commonwealth.

[1] See *Capital*, I, pp. 610-11.   [2] See Marx, *Class Struggles in France*, 1848-50.

For the time being there remains, along with the imperfect social organization of material production in the structure of the present bourgeois society, also the "reversed" form in which the social relations of men are now reflected as mere relations of things. There remain unchanged, even in the newest "as good as Socialism" models of a planned and steered State-Capitalism, and there will remain so long as the products of labour are produced as commodities, all the fetish-categories of bourgeois economics : commodity, money, capital, wage-labour, increasing and decreasing total value of production and of export, profit-making capacity of industries, credits, etc., in short, all that which Marx in his philosophic phase called "human self-alienation," and in his scientific phase, "fetishism of commodity production." In spite of appearances such a system of production is not in the last analysis governed by a collective will of the associated workers but by the blind necessities of a fetishistic "Law of Value."

The apparent *Fetish Character of the Commodity* and with it the apparent validity of a fetishistic *Law of Value*, will not disappear—nor will the economic crises and depressions and the various forms of periodical and chronic mass unemployment, wars and civil wars cease to plague the modern "Civilized World," till the present mode of commodity production is entirely destroyed and human labour organized in a direct socialistic mode of production. "For this, however, a material groundwork is required, or a set of material conditions which are themselves the spontaneous outgrowth of a long and painful process of development."[1]

[1] See *Capital*, I, p. 46.

CHAPTER X

COMMON MISUNDERSTANDINGS OF THE MARXIAN DOCTRINE OF
VALUE AND SURPLUS VALUE

THE idea that there be an *equality* inherent in all kinds of labour, by which economists are entitled to regard *qualitatively different kinds* of labour such as the labour performed by the spinner, the weaver, the blacksmith, or the farm-hand, as *quantitatively different portions* of a total quantity of general "labour" is so little the discovery of a natural condition underlying the production and exchange of commodities, that this "equality" is, on the contrary, brought into existence by the social fact that under the conditions prevailing in present-day capitalist "commodity production" all labour products are produced as commodities for such exchange. In fact, *this "equality" appears nowhere else than in the "value" of the commodities so produced and exchanged.* The full development of the economic theory of labour value coincided with a stage of the historical development, when human labour had long ceased to be, as it were, "organically" connected with either the individual or with small productive communities and henceforth under the new bourgeois banner of Freedom of Trade, every particular kind of labour was treated as equivalent to every other particular kind of labour. It was just the advent of those particular historical conditions that was expressed by the classical economists when they traced back in an ever more consistent manner the "value" appearing in the exchange of commodities to the quantities of labour incorporated therein, though most of them actually believed that they had thus disclosed a truly "natural" law applying to every reasonable productive society formed by human beings when they have reached their age of maturity and enlightenment. There is, in spite of this vague idea of a "natural" equality lingering in the minds of some early bourgeois economists, no validity

151

whatever in the naive objection which now for almost a century has been raised against the objective theory of value by pointing to the real inequality of the various kinds of labour. Those well-meaning defenders of Marxism who, on the other hand, attempt to correct the apparent "flaw" in the Marxian doctrine of labour value by actually trying to represent the useful labour in every particular labour product as a strictly measurable quantity, merely present the sad picture of one who holds a sieve beneath the billy-goat while another keeps busy to milk him. According to Marx's critical teaching, the natural difference of the various kinds of productive human labour is by no means wiped out by the fact (unquestionable in itself) that a major part of the differences in rank, presumably existing between many kinds of labour in present-day bourgeois society, rest on "mere illusions, or, to say the least, on differences, which have long ceased to be real and continue only by a social tradition."[1] The particular kinds of labour performed in the production of the various useful things are, according to Marx, *by their very nature different*, and just this difference is a necessary premise for the exchange of the labour products and the social division of labour brought about by it. Only on the basis of a qualitative division of labour arising spontaneously from the variety of social needs and the variety of kinds of useful labour performed to meet those needs, arises, by a further development, a possibility that this qualitative difference, for the purpose of an ever wider exchange, may gradually yield its place to the merely quantitative differences which the various kinds of labour possess as so many portions of the total quantity of the social labour expended in the production of all products consumed (or otherwise disposed of) at a given time within a given society. It is just this condition which has been first expressed theoretically by the "law of value" as formulated by the classical economists.[2] Those minor followers in the wake of the great scientific founders of Political

[1] See *Capital*, I, p. 160-61, footnote 18.   [2] *Ibid*, pp. 39-40.

152

Economy, no longer accustomed to such audacity of scientific thought, who have later pathetically bewailed the "violent abstraction" by which the classical economists and Marxism, in tracing back the value relations of commodities to the amounts of labour incorporated therein, have "equated the unequal," must be reminded of the fact that this "violent abstraction" does not result from the theoretical definitions of economic science, but from the real character of capitalist commodity production. *The commodity is a born leveller.* Over against this, it appears as a relatively unimportant fault in the construction of existing capitalist society that the theoretical principle of exchange of equal quantities of labour is no longer strictly realized in each single case but only, perhaps, on a rough average.

Contrary to all adverse opinions prevailing in one or the other camp, it was never the intention of Marx to descend, from the general idea of value as expounded in the first volume of *Capital*, by means of ever closer determinants to that direct determination of the price of commodities, for which at a later time Walras and Pareto set up their delusive systems of *n* millions of equations into which we need only introduce the required *n* millions of constants, to calculate with mathematical accuracy the price of a definite individual commodity at a given time. It was a catastrophical misunderstanding of Marx's economic theory when, after the appearance of the second and third volumes of *Capital*, the whole dogmatic dispute between the bourgeois critics of Marx and the orthodox Marxists centred round the question whether, and in what sense, the transformation of the "values" of the commodities into "production prices," by means of the intermediary concept of an "average rate of profits," is consistent with the general definition of "value" in the first volume. As shown by the MSS. and by the correspondence which were later published it was long before the appearance of the first volume, that Marx had finally laid down the principle that the "production prices" of commodities produced by capitals of various organic constitution can no longer be identical with their "values" as determined by the "law of value," either in individual cases or on the average, but are only a compound result of that main factor along with a series of other factors.[1] The particular importance of the law of value within Marx's theory, then, has nothing to do with a direct fixation of the prices of commodities by their value. It would be nearer the truth to say that the working of this law appears in the general *development* of the prices of commodities, in which the continuous depreciation in value of the commodities, effected by the ever-increasing productivity of social labour consequent upon the further accumulation of capital, constitutes the decisive factor. The ultimate meaning of this law as shown in its working by Marx in all three volumes of *Capital* does not consist, however, in supplying a theoretical basis for the practical calculations of the business man seeking his private advantage, or for the economico-political measures taken by the bourgeois statesman concerned with the general maintenance and furtherance of the capitalist surplus-making machinery. The final scientific purpose of the Marxian theory is rather to reveal "*the economic law of motion of modern society,*" and that means at the same time *the law of its historical development.*[2] Even more clearly was this expressed by the Marxist Lenin when he said that "the direct purpose of a Marxist investigation consists in the disclosure of all forms of the antagonism and exploitation existing in present-day capitalist society in order to aid the proletariat to do away with them."[3]

Similarly, the *doctrine of surplus value* which is usually regarded as the more particularly socialist section of Marx's economic theory is not either a simple economic exercise in calculation

[1] See Marx's letter to Engels, 27.7.1867 (MEGA, III, iii, pp. 403-04).
[2] See *Preface* to first edition of *Capital*, 1867.
[3] See Lenin, "*Who are the 'Friends of the People' and how do they fight against the Social Democrats?*" 1894, Collected Works, I (Russian).

which serves to check a fraudulent statement of value received and expended by capital in its dealing with the workers, or a moral lesson drawn from economics for the purpose of reclaiming from capital the diverted portion of the "full product of the worker's labour." The Marxian doctrine, as an economic theory, starts rather from the opposite principle that the industrial capitalist under "normal" conditions acquires the labour power of the wage labourers by means of a respectable and businesslike bargain, whereby the labourer receives the full equivalent of the "commodity" sold by him, that is, of the "labour power" incorporated in himself. The advantage gained by the capitalist in this business derives not from economics but from his privileged social position as the monopolist owner of the material means of production which permits him to exploit for the production of commodities in his workshop the specific *use value* of a labour power which he has purchased at its economic *"value"* (exchange value). Between the value of the new commodities produced by the use of the labour power in the workshop, and the prices paid for this labour to its sellers, there is, according to Marx, no economic or other rationally determinable relation whatever. The measure of value produced by the workers in the shape of their labour products over and above the equivalent of their wages, i.e., the *mass of "surplus labour"* expended by them in producing this "surplus value ;" and the quantitative relation between this surplus labour and the necessary labour, i.e., the *"rate of surplus value"* or the *"rate of exploitation"* holding good for a particular time and a particular country do not result from any exact economic calculation. They result from a battle between social classes which assumes sharper and sharper forms just because no objective limits are set for the increase of the rate and mass of the surplus value under the conditions of an ever-increasing accumulation of capital at one pole, and the simultaneous accumulation of misery at the opposite pole of society.

CHAPTER XI

POLITICAL Economy is, through the Marxian criticism, deprived of its extravagant claims and referred back to its historical and social context. It is transformed (and this is the "Copernican turn" of the Marxian *Critique of Political Economy*) from an absolute and timeless science into one which is historically and socially conditioned. According to Marx, Political Economy is a bourgeois science which springs from the particular historical form of the bourgeois mode of production and is its ideological supplement. From this critical conception of Political Economy results a thorough change in the mode of validity of all its categories and propositions. On the one hand, because of the fetish character which attaches itself to all economic categories beginning with the fundamental categories of commodity and of money, these categories do not apply to any real and directly given object ; the presumed "objects" of economics are themselves nothing but materially disguised expressions for the definite relations into which men enter among themselves, in the social production of their means of existence. On the other hand, the economic categories, in spite of their fetish character or, perhaps just because of it, represent the necessary form in which that particular historical and historically transitory state of an "imperfect sociality," which is characteristic of the bourgeois production relations, is reflected in the social consciousness of this epoch. They are, as Marx said, "socially valid and, therefore, objective thought-forms which apply to the production-relations peculiar to this one historically determined mode of social production, to wit, commodity production."[1] They are, as will be further shown in the third

[1] See *Capital*, I, p. 42.

part of this book, inseparably connected with the real existence of the bourgeois mode of production and the "social laws" which hold good for this particular epoch of society. As long as that material foundation of the existing bourgeois society is only attacked and shaken, but not completely overthrown, through the revolutionary proletarian struggle, also the socially entrenched thought-forms of the bourgeois epoch can only be criticized and not definitely superseded by the revolutionary theory of the proletariat. The critique of Political Economy, which Marx began in *Capital*, can therefore only be completed by the proletarian revolution, i.e., by a real change of the present bourgeois mode of production and of the forms of consciousness pertaining to it. It is only after the full accomplishment of this revolution that, in the further development of the Communist society, all "fetishism of commodity production" and the whole "fetishistic" science of Political Economy will be finally merged into a direct social theory and practice of the associated producers.[1]

Until that time, the terms and propositions by which Political Economy had expressed the scientific results of its investigation into the material foundations of the present order of society, in a manner befitting its period in spite of their fetish form, remain valid even for that materialistic science by which Marx and his followers have criticized the standpoint of bourgeois economy from the new historical and theoretical standpoint of a new social class. Notwithstanding his revolutionary criticism of all preceding Political Economy, Marx remained, in his theoretical work, first and foremost, an *economic investigator*. He did not dissipate economics in history, sociology, and in the Utopias but, on the contrary, he condensed the general and indefinite form of the traditional historical and social studies into a materialistic investigation of their economic foundations. He was less and less disposed, the farther he went in his exact scientific analysis of the bourgeois mode of production, to leave aside

[1] See Marx, *Marginal Notes to the Programme of the German Labour Party*, 1877 (Neue Zeit, IX, pp. 566-67).

that exceedingly important material, available in the results of classic bourgeois economy, and which only needs further logical development and critical utilization. Nor did he want to leave it to the minor disciples of the great classical economists, who misinterpreted it for the purpose of a social apology for the existing capitalist system.

This positive attitude of Marx towards economic science is evident in his relation to all other standpoints which were represented within bourgeois and, to a certain extent, also within socialist science at his time.

Marx stood, in spite of his historical criticism of the "eternal laws of nature" of traditional Political Economy, in a much sharper contrast to the so-called "Historical School" which, by its dispersal of all definite economic concepts, represented nothing but a self-destruction and abdication of economics as a science.

Similarly, already in his first philosophical period, he had opposed the ideological manner, in which such writers as Bruno Bauer, Stirner and Feuerbach had considered all human "self-alienation" as a mere philosophical category. He had emphasized the fact that the actual "self-alienation" of the wage labourer who sells his own labour power to the capitalistic owner of the means of production can not be abolished by a mere process of thought, but only by a social action. In the same realistic mood he dismissed with contempt, in his later period, that superficial "sociological" theory which, in contrast to the "economic realism" of the classicists, "regarded value as nothing more than a conventional form, or, rather, as the ghost of such a form."[1] (We may add in passing that this brief remark which Marx seventy years ago bestowed on the views held at that time by a few remaining supporters of a "restored Mercantile system" is still very pertinent, and perhaps particularly so to-day, as a criticism of the theoretical suggestions and practical schemes

[1] See *Capital*, I, pp. 47-48, footnote 32.

disseminated by the modern "money theorists" and "credit reformers," who likewise look upon commodity prices and more particularly upon "money" as arbitrary, conventional, and manageable forms.) While Marx and Engels had no quarrel with such practical exponents of revolutionary force as Blanqui, they pointed at every possible opportunity to the scientific emptiness of so-called sociological "theories of violence,"[1] They were not deceived by the clamorous ways of those would-be "progressive" and even half "socialistically-minded" people who, candidly unconscious of the real motive force of historical development and deliberately ignoring all economics with the possible exception of a few general and unchangeable economic "laws of nature," endeavoured to trace the existing forms of production, of class relationship and other disagreeable facts to pure force, politics, etc., in order to appeal from such "brute" forms of violence to the organizing power of reason, of justice, of humanity, or similar classless immaterialities. Marx and Engels, as against such "sociological" despisers of economics, always affirmed their allegiance to the deeper and richer historical knowledge of bourgeois society which is contained in the economic concept of "value" and in the analyses based on it by the bourgeois classicists.

Finally, Marx, whose "materialistic" and scientific socialism arose in direct contrast to the "doctrinary" and "Utopian" socialism of the preceding phase of the workers' movement, remained throughout his life a sworn enemy of all merely "imaginary" *constructions* to a degree that already on this ground the tenets of economic science which in spite of their formal deficiencies are at least based on definite historical and social facts, were for him of an incomparably greater significance than any future type existing as yet only in the thought of an individual reformer.

This holds good even for the rare cases where Marx himself

[1] See e.g., the three fulminating sections under this heading in Engels' *Anti-Dühring*, 1878.

in the course of his exposition endeavoured to elucidate his theoretical standpoint by confronting the present-day capitalistic commodity production with some other, past historical or possible future, forms of social production. It applies above all to four short paragraphs of the section dealing with the *"Fetish Character of the Commodity and its Secret"*[1] in which Marx, to dispel "all the mystery of the world of commodities, all the enchantment and bewitchment which befog the products of labour in a system based on commodity production," calls up successively four different social modes of production : that of Robinson Crusoe (the lonely islander), the feudal mode of production of the Middle Ages, the patriarchial management of a peasant family working on the land, and, finally, "for a change," an association of free men who work with common means of production and consciously expend their many individual labour powers as a combined social labour power. Similarly, the detailed description of one of those ancient small Indian communities in which "there is a social division of labour, but the products of labour do not become commodities,"[2] is not of any particular significance for the economic theory of *Capital* though it is more important with regard to the broader aspects of the materialistic theory of history and society. In the particular context in which it appears within the exposition of Marx's fundamental economic concepts in *Capital*, it serves only as a supplementary historical illustration of the theoretical contrast between the *division of labour inside the workshop and the division of labour in society as a whole*.[3]

The main theoretical purpose of all such "quasi-historical" comparisons is the same which is served, in another way, by Marx's favourite comparison of the economic "fetishism of the commodity" with the "reflection of the real world in religion."[4] Just as a real criticism of religion must not content itself with

[1] See *Capital*, I, pp. 43-51.   [2] *Ibid*, pp. 8 and 322 *et seq.*
[3] *Ibid*, I, pp. 8 and 315-324.
[4] See, for example, pp. 39 and 45-46.

finding out, through scientific analysis, the earthly kernel of the foggy forms of the religious phantasms, so a criticism of the economic categories is imperfect as long as it restricts itself to a disclosure of the actual material conditions underlying their apparent "fetishistic" form. *Materialistic criticism of religion* is aware of the fact that the ideological reflection of the real world in religion cannot be totally dissolved until the practical conditions of every day offer to the human beings concerned a continuous display of perfectly intelligible and reasonable relations both between man and nature and between men and men. Similarly, the life process of society, i.e., material production does not strip off its mystical veil until it is transformed into the result of the conscious and self-controlled activities of freely associated men.[1] Till then a *scientific critique of Political Economy* must supplement its theoretical analysis of the fetish form of the economic categories by a positive understanding of their transitory historical necessity and rationality, and must utilize the real knowledge contained therein for a materialistic investigation of the social development going on within the present historical epoch.

Only in some passages of *Capital* did Marx replace the economic categories hitherto applied in the presentation of his theory by a direct historical description of the bourgeois mode of production and the real conflict of the social classes concealed behind the two economic categories "capital" and "wage-labour."[2] Here belong, for instance, two passages in the eighth chapter of the first volume where Marx winds up a detailed discussion of the economically undetermined and indeterminable limits of the working day by the statement that "the regulation of the working day is, in real history, the outcome of a protracted civil war between the capitalist class and the working class," and calls upon the workers "to put their heads together

[1] See Marx, *Capital*, I, p. 46.
[2] See *Introduction* to the author's edition of *Capital*, 1932, pp. 19 *et seq.*

161

for protection against the worm gnawing at their vitals and, by united action as a class, to compel the passing of a law which will put in place of the pompous catalogue of the 'inalienable rights of man' the modest Magna Charta of a legally limited working day that shall at length make it clear when the time which the worker sells is ended, and when his own begins."[1]

Here belong many other not very bulky, but significant passages leading up to the famous investigation of the "*So-Called Primitive Accumulation*" which, together with the immediately following analysis of *Modern Colonization* finally concludes the case of Socialism against Capitalism as presented by Marx in his theory.[2]

Marx has in the preceding chapters fully described the economic nature of the existing mode of production. He has gone through the economic analysis of value and labour, of surplus value and surplus labour, of reproduction, of the accumulation both of the individual capital and of the sum total of the capitals available in a given society. When thus all has been said that can be said about the origin of capital in terms of economic science, there still remains an unsolved residue in form of the question, "Whence came the first capital?"[3] Whence arose, before all capitalistic production, the first capitalistic relation between an exploiting capitalist and the exploited wage-labourers? Whence descended the Vampire that preys upon the toiling masses of modern society and will not loose its hold "so long as there is a muscle, a nerve, a drop of blood to be exploited?"[4] This question—unanswered by the bourgeois economists and, indeed, unanswerable economically — has already been repeatedly examined by Marx in the foregoing exposition.[5] It is now taken up again to be treated no longer as an economic question at all. Instead, the problem is grimly and

[1] See *Capital*, I, pp. 196 and 262-66.
[2] *Ibid*, xxiv and xxv.   [3] *Ibid*, pp. 679 *et seq.*
[4] *Ibid*, pp. 265-66 and the 1850 essay by Engels, there quoted.
[5] See *Capital*, I, pp. 531, 545, 588.

thoroughly cleared up in a direct historical investigation and solved by a practical rather than a theoretical conclusion. The *"Historical Tendency of Capitalistic Accumulation,"* as illustrated by the classic example of the capitalist production in England, leads to a result which, if it emanates with "the inevitability of a process of nature" from the objective development of capitalism itself, yet requires a practical social act to set it free. "The last hour of capitalistic private property strikes. The expropriators are expropriated."[1] A similar line of argument prevails throughout the remaining parts of Marx's work. Just as the first book of *Capital* actually leads up to the outbreak of the proletarian revolution, so the whole of the Marxian theory as presented in the three books of *Capital*, was meant to result in the historical event of the revolutionary class war.[2]

But even at these extreme points where the revolutionary principle is definitely laid open in *Capital*, Marx did not entirely abandon economic theory. He merely revealed in a more outspoken manner the historical and social barrier which was already reflected in the "fetish-character" of the economic categories and on account of which an uncritical adoption of those categories was excluded from the new socialistic theory from the outset. Some end and border problems of Political Economy which were now first discovered from the new standpoint of the proletarian class, so far transcended the horizon of the bourgeois economist that they could no longer be approached, much less solved within the realm of the economic science. The categories by which the classical economists had elucidated the material foundations of the then arising bourgeois society, were scientifically sufficient for the time. With certain critical amendments, they represent even now, within

---

[1] See *Capital*, I, pp. 726 *et seq.*

[2] See Marx's letter to Engels of 30.4.1868 (MEGA, III, iv, p. 49) and the outlines for the intended continuation of the final chapter (chap. lii), on *Classes*, of which only a few pages were worked out in the Marxian MSS) as sketched by Engels in his *Preface* to the third vol. of *Capital*, pp. IX-X.

limited fields and for short periods of time, a valuable instrument for the scientific analysis of definite sections of the bourgeois mode of production. However, they prove to be unsuitable for a more extensive investigation which embraces the total historical development of bourgeois commodity production, including its origin and decay, and its revolutionary transition to a direct social organization of production. They are, as Marx and Engels emphasized in their later period, even more unsuitable for a comprehensive materialistic history of human society, looking backwards to primæval times and forwards to the fully developed Communist Society.

PART THREE
HISTORY

CHAPTER I

THE MATERIALISTIC CONCEPTION OF HISTORY

MARX and Engels never considered their new principle of economic and social research as more than a new scientific approach to a strictly empirical investigation of the historical development of the modern capitalistic mode of production. Marx referred to it in 1859 as a "general result" at which he had arrived during the first period of his economic research and which, once gained, served as a "guiding principle" to his subsequent studies.[1] Twenty years later he refuted the erroneous conclusion of the Russian sociologist Michaelovsky who had misinterpreted the general description of the "Historical Tendency of Capital Accumulation" in Marx's *Capital* as a "suprahistorique" principle, that without a previous investigation of the actual historical facts could be applied to any other period and indeed to the whole history of human society. He pointed out that that description, despite its general form, was merely a "résumé" of the materials which had already been examined in detail in the previous chapters and thus was nothing more than a *historical sketch of the rise of capitalism in Western Europe.*[2] His attitude was fully shared by Friedrich Engels who about the same time opposed the old traditional conception of the historical process which "knew nothing of the class struggles based upon material interests, in fact, of no material interests at all," and dealt with such topics as production and all economic conditions only accessorily, as "subordinate elements of the history of culture." He confronted that old "*idealistic conception of history*"

[1] See *Preface* 1859.
[2] See Marx's letter to the editor of *Otetshestvenneye Sapiski*, written at the end of 1877—first published in Russian in the *Viestnik Narodnoj Voli*, 1886, and re-translated into German for the New York "*Volkszeitung*" 1887; this translation has since taken the place of the lost original MS.

KARL MARX

with the new principle of the proletarian science and, incidentally, gave the "Materialistic Conception of History"[1] its later and universally accepted name. This name, by the way, was never applied to it by Marx himself who was quite content to describe it as a "materialistic and thus scientific method."[2]

Just as any other experimental natural and social science, the Marxian theory of society cannot take its departure from a preconceived and dogmatic principle ; even less so because the science of Marx is a "critical" rather than a positive science. He criticizes theoretically the doctrines of bourgeois social science which are no longer tenable, just as during the same period the existing forms of bourgeois society which have become untenable at the present stage of historical development are practically criticized and transformed by the revolutionary action of the working class.

Even where Marx departs from that purely critical position, he does not lay down any general propositions as to the essential nature of all society but merely describes the particular conditions and developmental tendencies inherent in the historical form of contemporary bourgeois society.

The critical principle of Marx's *social science* was during the subsequent development of Marxism converted into a general *social philosophy*. From this first misconception, it was only one step further to the idea that the historical and economic science of Marx must be based on the broader foundation not only of a social philosophy but even of an all-comprehensive "materialistic philosophy" embracing both nature and society, or a general philosophical interpretation of the universe. Thus the definitely scientific forms which the real kernel of the philosophical materialism of the 18th century had assumed in the historical materialism of Marx were ultimately carried back to what Marx himself had once unmistakably repudiated as "the philosophical phrases of the Materialists about matter."[3]

[1] See Engels, *"Anti-Dühring,"* 1878.
[2] See *Capital*, I, pp. 335-36, footnote 89.   [3] See MEGA, I, v, p. 83.

168

Marx's materialistic science, being a strictly empirical investigation into definite historical forms of society, does not need a philosophical support. This most important point made in Marx's historical materialism was later missed even by those "orthodox" Marx-interpreters who themselves combated with the utmost energy all attempts made by the later critics, within and without the Marxist camp, to "revise Marxism" by basing it on some or other contemporary non-materialistic philosophy. In their painstaking efforts to protect the true Marxist materialism from what they quite correctly regarded as an undesirable dilution of the genuine Marxian thought, they overlooked the fact that that most highly developed form of materialistic science which is embodied in Marx's empirical investigation of society is not only far in advance of all idealistic philosophy, but of all philosophical thought whatever. They wanted to strengthen the materialistic character of the Marxian science by giving it a philosophical interpretation. They have, in fact, only superfluously re-introduced their own backward philosophical attitudes into a theory which Marx had previously transformed from a philosophy into a veritable science. It was the historical fate of the Marx-orthodoxy that its opponents, while repulsing the attacks of the "revisionists" ultimately arrived, on all important issues, at the same standpoint as that taken by their adversaries. For example, the leading representative of this school, the philosophical materialist and orthodox Marxist Plechanov, in all his eager search for that "materialistic philosophy" which might be the true foundation of Marxism, finally hit upon the idea of presenting Marxism as "a form of Spinoza's philosophy, freed by Feuerbach from its theological additions."[1]

While both schools of the philosophical interpreters of Marxism ultimately coupled Marx's materialistic theory with a

[1] See Plechanov, *Fundamental Problems of Marxism* (Russian, 1908; German 1910 and 1929) and, against that wrong conception of Marxism, Marx's and Engels' own statements in *The Holy Family* (MEGA, I, iii, pp. 308 *et seq.*, 313 *et seq.*) and *The German Ideology* (MEGA, I, v, pp. 76 *et seq.*)

philosophical, that is, an idealistic form of thought, there is still a considerable difference between them historically and theoretically. The association of Marx with Spinoza connects him with an early bourgeois philosophy, which, while in form idealistic, comprised also the germ of the future materialistic mode of thought. On the other hand, those modern philosophical improvisators who wanted to fill a presumed gap in Marx's system with Kant's, Mach's, Dietzgen's, or any other kind of non-materialistic philosophy, utterly ignore the whole historical and theoretical situation.[1] The only reason why the materialistic philosophers Marx and Engels, up from a certain point in their development, turned their backs upon every philosophy, even the materialistic philosophy (leaving far behind such less consistent anti-philosophical gospels as those of Feuerbach and Moses Hess who for a time had preceded them in this tendency) is the fact that they wanted to go one step further and to outbid the materialism of philosophy by a direct materialistic science and practice.[2] This did not prevent them from opposing, in their own scientific work, every *non-materialistic* standpoint, no matter in what disguise it appeared. They expressly included in these "non-materialistic" or "not univocally materialistic" standpoints, also the whole modern positivism (as represented by Comte and others) which seems on the surface to be closely related to their anti-philosophical materialism, and that "agnostic" attitude which is derived by modern scientists from Hume's philosophy and which in Marx's lifetime was represented in England by Thomas Huxley.[3] The fight against all shades of philosophical

[1] See the author's *Marxism and Philosophy*, second edition 1930, pp. 21 and 53, and footnote 8.
[2] See Marx and Engels, *German Ideology*, 1845-46 (MEGA, I, v; particularly pp. 8 *et seq.* 24, 76 *et seq.*, 215-16). See also Marx's later statement in *Preface* 1859, that he and Engels, in that earlier work, "worked out together the contrast between their view and the ideology of German philosophy and, in fact, settled accounts with their former philosophical conscience." For a more detailed discussion see the author's *Marxism and Philosophy*, pp. 67 *et seq.* and pp. 8 *et seq.*
[3] See Marx's letter to Engels of 12.12.1866 (MEGA, III, iii, p. 368).

idealism became even more important when, in the period immediately after Marx's death "classical German philosophy underwent a kind of revival mainly in England and Scandinavia, but also in Germany."[1] That is why now even an altogether scientifically and empirically minded Marxist like Friedrich Engels, rehearsed the philosophical materialism of his youth and set himself to work out once more, against the new obscurantist tendencies which were rapidly gaining ground among the various schools of contemporary bourgeois philosophy, the persisting affinity between the materialistic science of Marxism and a general, and therefore in a certain sense "philosophical," materialistic view of the universe. The same reason applies in a later historical period, to the philosophical battles waged against the so-called "Empirio-Criticism" and other idealistic philosophies by the militant materialist Lenin.[2]

There is then, no reasonable doubt as to the affiliation of Marxism to the most definitely materialistic creed to be found in present-day philosophy and science. But the position is different in regard to the often recurring statement that Marx's *historical materialism* sprang directly from, and is still now theoretically dependent upon, one or another form of *philosophical materialism*, as for example the revolutionary bourgeois materialism of the 18th century, or the materialistic criticism of religion from Strauss to Feuerbach.

[1] See Engels' *Introduction to Ludwig Feuerbach and the End of Classical Philosophy*, 1888.
[2] See *Marxism and Philosophy*, pp. 27 *et seq.*

CHAPTER II

THE GENESIS OF HISTORICAL MATERIALISM

THERE is no doubt that Marx fully shared, for a time, the tremendous enthusiasm felt during the 40's by the whole school of Left Hegelians for the materialistic message of Feuerbach.[1] The influence exerted upon his theory by this experience may, perhaps, be best compared with that of Hume on Kant as summed up by the latter in the formula that "Hume aroused me from the dogmatic slumber." Yet there is an important difference in the degree to which Marx on the one hand, and the other Hegelians including Engels, were impressed by the particular form of materialism represented by Feuerbach. It is no wonder that Friedrich Engels who had suffered much in his childhood under the pietistic cant of the Wupper valley and had received his first lesson in philosophical materialism from the gospel criticism of the Hegelian David Friedrich Strauss and then passed from the disciple to the master discovering behind the idealistic formulæ of Hegel the germs of an altogether different atheistic and materialistic creed, was later decisively influenced by the outspoken materialism to which those germs were developed by Feuerbach.[2] It was certainly otherwise with Marx. He was brought up in a freethinking family and reached his ultimate materialistic standpoint by a much longer road through a study of Democritus and Epicurus, of the materialists of the 17th and 18th centuries, and finally through a detailed critical revision of the whole idealistic philosophy of Hegel. His progress toward materialism was indeed, from the begin-

[1] See the later testimony of Engels in his essay *On Feuerbach*, 1888.
[2] See the detailed references in Gustav Mayer's *Friedrich Engels*, 1933. See further the recent study by Reinhart Seeger on *Friedrich Engels, the Religious Development of a Late Pietist and Early Socialist*. (Christianity and Socialism, Sources and Studies, published by Ernst Barnikol, 1935).

172

ning and through all its phases, a progress to revolutionary materialistic politics.[1] He was already a revolutionary materialist in this political sense although still using the language of Hegel's idealism, when he raved against the *"reprobate materialism"* of the *Prussian State Gazette* which "in considering a Statute on the stealing of wood thought only of wood and did not solve that single and material task *politically*, i.e., not in connection with the reason and ethics of the State as a whole."[2] He was already a materialistic critic of all existing realizations of the State-idea when he reproached Hegel for "proceeding from the State to make man a subjective form of the State" instead of, "in the sense of modern democracy," proceeding from man to make the State an objective form of man. He described as early as this "democracy" as being "the general form of the State in which the formal principle is at the same time the *material* principle," and added the far-reaching remark that "the modern French have understood this to mean that in true democracy the political State must disappear."[3]

For all these reasons the materialistic rupture with all theological and philosophical idealism which was effected by Feuerbach in his book on the *Essence of Christendom*, 1841, and, even more powerfully, in his *Preliminary Theses on the Reform of Philosophy*, 1842, did not have that sweeping effect upon Marx that it had upon Engels and, even more persistently, upon Strauss, Bruno Bauer, etc., who, all through their lives, did not emerge from the phase of religious criticism. Thus becomes evident the real meaning of the sentence by which Marx in 1843 described the criticism of religion as "the premise of all criticism."[4] This oft-

[1] See Marx's thesis on *The Difference between Democritean and Epicurean Philosophy of Nature*. 1841, and the detailed report on the progress of his philosophical studies given by young Marx to his father in a letter of 10.11.1837 (MEGA, I, i, 1, pp. 1-144, and I, i, 2, pp. 213-21).
[2] See Marx's article *On the Debates of the 6th Rhineland Diet* in *Rheinische Zeitung* of 3.11.1842, No. 307 (MEGA I, 1, 1 ; p. 304).
[3] See MEGA, I, i, 1, p. 435.
[4] See Marx, *Introduction to a Critique of the Hegelian Philosophy of Law*, 1843 (MEGA, I, i, 1, p. 607).

quoted phrase had at the time when it was formulated by Marx under the conditions prevailing in Prussia after the change of government, besides its general theoretical a definite political significance. Marx proclaimed the attack of the bourgeois free-thinkers against the reactionary religious policy of the new régime to be the first phase of that "political movement" which beginning in 1840 was to lead up to the 1848 revolution. By the same reason a criticism restricted to religion lost the positive significance it had borne for a time as soon as that first phase was brought to a close by the "socialist ideas circulating in Germany since 1843." While in the first phase the "critique of religion" had served as a veil concealing the political aims of the speedily growing revolutionary movement of the early 40's, that movement had now reached a point at which, according to Marx, even a political struggle had become a mere transparent veil concealing the social struggle beneath.[1] Marx had already declared before and, in fact, in the very sentence in which he spoke of the criticism of religion as being "the premise of all criticism," that "the criticism of religion, for all practical purposes, has been concluded in Germany."[2] It is true that both he and Engels, one year later, reaffirmed their allegiance to the "real humanism" of Feuerbach ;[3] they did so with a view to retain an ally indispensable in the impending revolutionary fight. They did not, for that matter, retract their criticism of that "merely naturalistic, not historical and economic materialism" which was represented by Feuerbach then and at all later times.[4] Nor did they except Feuerbach from the final attack they directed during the following year against the whole of the Left Hegelians who still remained rooted in philosophical ground. Marx was by now definitely tired of "any criticism of religion

[1] See MEGA, I, iii, p. 287.   [2] *Ibid*, I, i, 1, p. 607.
[3] See Marx and Engels, *Holy Family*, 1844 (MEGA, I, iii, pp. 179, 316). See also the further acknowledgments to Feuerbach (not quite so un-restricted) in the draft Preface and text of the *Critique of National Economy* of the same year (MEGA, I, iii, pp. 35, 123, 151 *et seq*).
[4] See MEGA, I, iii, p. 327.

which does not go beyond its proper sphere."[1] That is to say, he had left religious criticism far behind and had progressed from the "premise" to its political and social consequences, from "criticism of heaven" to "criticism of earth," from "criticism of religion" to "criticism of law," from "criticism of theology" to "criticism of politics,"[2] and from there, in a subsequent stage, to a criticism of the still more earthly forms which the religious reflexion of the real world assumes in the economic sphere, i.e., of the "fetish character of the commodity world" and of the categories of Political Economy derived from it.[3]

A materialistic criticism of the prevailing *social and political conditions* could not be built upon the mainly naturalistic materialism which had been professed by Feuerbach.[4] Feuerbach had conceived of the human being as "an abstract entity inherent in the single individual." He had not, like Marx, described it as "the ensemble of the social conditions."[5] He understood the world "only in the form of an *object* or of contemplation." It was, however, of decisive importance for historical materialism to understand the given reality and its development also from a subjective viewpoint as "a human sensual activity, i.e., practice," and thus to conceive of human action itself as an "objective activity."[6] The naturalistic materialism of Feuerbach which "excluded the historical process," was not capable of fulfilling that most important task even in its own peculiar and limited sphere, the criticism of religion. Only "historical materialism" which on an economic, historical, and social (not only natural and biological) basis "explains the active behaviour of man

[1] See *German Ideology*, 1845-46 (MEGA, I, v, p. 214).
[2] See MEGA, I, i, 1, p. 608.
[3] See above pp. 131 *et seq.*
[4] See Marx's letter to Ruge of 13.3.1843: "Feuerbach's aphorisms are unsatisfactory in my opinion only in this respect that he refers too much to nature and too little to politics."
[5] See the sixth of Marx's *Theses on Feuerbach* of 1845, posthumously published by Engels as an Appendix to his *On Feuerbach*, 1888. (Now also MEGA, I, v, pp. 533 *et seq*).
[6] *Ibid*, p. 533, first thesis.

KARL MARX

towards nature, the direct production of his life, and thus also of his social conditions and of the ideas arising from them," provides a truly materialistic development of the religious ideas. "All history of religion which ignores this material basis is uncritical."[1] It was in this context that Marx added the statement quoted in a previous chapter that "it is, in fact, much easier to find by analysis the secular kernel of the religious mysteries than, conversely, to derive their exalted forms from the prevailing real conditions. The latter is the unique materialistic and therefore the scientific method."[2]

While the "Feuerbach cult" which Marx had shared with the other young Hegelians for an extremely short time, did on the whole not leave a deep mark on his materialistic theory,[3] he was much more impressed by that earlier form of bourgeois materialism which had been inaugurated by "the English and French" in the course of the 17th and 18th centuries. The attitude of Marx and Engels to the different phases of bourgeois social theory and economics which we have dealt with in the First and Second Parts of this book exactly repeats itself in their attitude towards the different historical phases of bourgeois materialism. They dismissed with utter contempt that "shallow and vulgarized form in which 18th century materialism continues to-day in the minds of the natural scientists and physicians, and which was preached on their lecture tours in the 50's by Büchner, Vogt, and Moleschott."[4] On the other hand, they always regarded their new proletarian and revolutionary mate-

[1] See *Capital*, I, pp. 335-36, footnote 89.   [2] See above, pp. 160-161.
[3] See Marx's remarks on this subject in *German Ideology* (MEGA, I, v, p. 85) and in his letter to Engels of 24.4.1867 (MEGA. III, iii, p. 383). See further Engels' letters to Marx of 19.11.1844, 19.8.1846, and of the middle of October, 1846 (MEGA, III, i, pp. 7, 27-28, 44-47) and Marx's final judgment on Feuerbach in his letter to the editor of the *Social Democrat* of 24.1.1865: "Compared with Hegel, Feuerbach is poor. Nevertheless he was epoch-making *after* Hegel because he emphasized certain points unpleasant to the Christian conscience and important for the progress of criticism, which Hegel had left in a mystical chiaroscuro."
[4] See Engels, *On Feuerbach*, 1888.

176

rialism as a continuation and more highly developed stage of that classical bourgeois materialism which had formed the driving force of the bourgeoisie in its revolutionary epoch and had then already temporarily begun to branch off directly into socialism and communism.[1] This relation, however, is more of a general affiliation than a definite adoption of methods and results. On the entirely new field now opened by the extension of the materialistic principle to the historical and social sciences, and under the changed historical conditions of the 19th century, Marx and Engels could no longer utilize the primitive forms of those early forerunners for their own research, although they went on to admire and to praise the bourgeois materialism of the 18th century for its militant revolutionary tendency.

The bourgeois materialists had not developed any adequate principles for the historical and social studies. They had, indeed, boldly proclaimed their materialistic principle as fundamental for all fields of existence and knowledge. They did not dream of the half-heartedness of present-day natural scientists who actually apply a materialistic principle within the limited branch in which they happen to do their professional scientific work, but carefully avoid any further extension of that materialism and cheerfully regard themselves (to use an expression applied to Feuerbach by Engels) as "materialists underneath and idealists on top." Yet even the early bourgeois materialists had in fact directed their attention mainly to the field which of necessity attracted them because of its importance for modern industry, the very basis of bourgeois society. Thus they had worked out primarily a materialistic science of nature, and dealt with "society" only in passing as a secondary part of the natural world. The more definite and more threatening the forms of the proletarian class-movement became in the further development of bourgeois society, the more was bourgeois materialism driven back from the thorny ground of "society" to "nature"

[1] See Marx, *Holy Family* (MEGA, I, iii, pp. 300-310).

as a field of scientific research. The bourgeois social science of the 19th and 20th centuries, in forgetting its revolutionary character generally, also forgot the materialism of its youthful phase and was able to reproduce it, if at all, only in the spasmodic and counter-revolutionary form, in which it appears for instance in Pareto's "materialistic" doctrine of ideologies.

Bourgeois materialism has revolutionized the natural sciences. The proletarian materialism of Marx and Engels proposed from the outset to subject the historical and social world to the same materialistic principle. Just as the materialism of natural science had built up its theoretical form in a critical fight against the surviving remainders of the theological metaphysics of the Middle Ages, so did historical and social materialism work out its new theoretical form by opposing that new metaphysics which in the meantime had settled on the field neglected by the old materialism, i.e., of historical and social phenomena, and had found its temporary conclusion in the German idealistic philosophy from Kant to Hegel.[1]

Marx found hidden beneath the idealistic speculative forms of Hegel's Philosophy of Law, History, Æsthetics, Religion, etc., of Logic and History of Philosophy, just that which he had not been able to find anywhere else in the whole of past and contemporary philosophy and science : namely, a methodical starting point for an empirical investigation of the so-called "spiritual nature of man," i.e., the realm of *history* or *society* as opposed to *nature*. The first importance of Hegel's philosophy for Marx's materialist science derives from the fact that here the sphere of "nature" had been confronted for the first time with the new sphere of the social relations of men as an equally comprehensive Universe of Research, both to be ultimately subordinated to one and the same supreme principle of knowledge. There is, of course, the difference that for Hegel that ultimate principle had been spiritual, while for Marx it was material.

[1] See the first of Marx's *Theses on Feuerbach* 1845 (MEGA, I, v, p. 533).

Hegel started from the "idea." Marx, on the contrary, in all his philosophical, juridical, and political studies took his start from a strictly empirical principle. He approached the historical, social, and practical world of man with the firm decision to investigate this so-called "world of the mind" which until then had been treated as something essentially different from physical and material nature, with the same "precision" which had been applied for several centuries by the great scientists to their study of physical nature. In so doing he carried out the programme which he had first formulated as a student of nineteen years when he was still inspired by the "idealism of Kant and Fichte," but just on the verge of succumbing to the lure of the great Hegelian philosophy. It was at that time, that young Karl Marx confessed to his alarmed father that he had now resolved "to plunge into the sea once more," but this time "with a definite intention of finding the nature of mind to be just as necessary, concrete, and tightly rounded as the nature of physics."[1] Hegel had indeed introduced into the investigation of the history of society and of the so-called "mind," somewhat more of the empirical attitude of the scientist who aims at a precise description and definition of really existing and verifiable connections than up to that time had been usual with the idealistic philosophers, adherents of the "organic" theory of the State, and the whole of the so-called "historical school." It was just this fact which definitely won over young Marx to the Hegelian philosophy, and held him under its spell for a considerable period of his life. He adhered, in truth, from the very beginning only to the "natural scientist" of society whom he had discovered beneath the mystifying disguise of the philosophical explorer of the human mind. He left Hegel at once when he felt able to represent in a direct and rational way those material connections between men and things, and between men and men which

[1] See Marx's letter to his father of 10.11.1837 (MEGA, I, i, 2, pp. 218-19).

formed the real contents hidden under an apparent speculative connection of ideas. The real contribution of Hegel to a materialistic investigation of society was that he had seen this material connection, in an idealistic form, and made it the subject of a philosophico-scientific exposition.

Hegel's philosophical system, the latest and most complete elaboration of that "natural system of the sciences of the mind" by which the theologico-metaphysical system of the Middle Ages had been replaced during the practical and theoretical struggles of the previous centuries, can be traced everywhere in the materialistic scheme of society. In an as comprehensive though idealistic and not materialistic sense had already Hegel (therewith translating into his "profound" philosophical slang the empirical discoveries of the English and French of the 17th and 18th centuries) distinguished between the two realms of reality, i.e., the "world of the mind" or "history" on the one hand, and the external world or "nature" on the other. He too, had subdivided that historical world into definite strata. Above the world of the "objective mind" (Family, Civil Society, State) there came the world of the "absolute mind" (Religion, Philosophy, Art).[1] He too, had regarded this world, at variance with itself, as a world in a process of development. There was only the characteristic difference that Hegel had superimposed on the *real* dependence of the "higher" strata of society upon the "lower," and on the *real* process of an historical development going on in time, of which he was fully aware, another reversed, and "idealistic" order of the universe in the shape of an imagined, *timeless development* and a similarly imagined *dependence of the lower forms of reality from the higher and more "spiritual" forms.* Hegel, too, had "dialectically" presented this development as being a "contradictory" process, in which the driving force is the negation of each position, the conflict resulting from that contradiction to be ultimately readjusted through the negation

[1] See Hegel *Encyclopædia*, Part III, §§ 2 and 3.

of the negation in a higher "synthesis." This order of the historico-social world, which in Hegel's philosophy "stood on its head," was put on its feet again by Marx through his "materialistic reversal of the Hegelian idealism."

Marx struck out of Hegel's scheme the *idea of the State* which Hegel had presented as the crowning conclusion and consummation of the mind standing in the world and consciously realizing itself within it. One must not confound the Hegelian "idea of the State" with that ordinary earthly phenomenon which with him is merely "the State as a civil society."[1] "One must not think of particular States, or particular institutions, one must consider rather the real God, the idea."[2]

When the real God was dethroned the whole kingdom fell. Just as the "State" and the "law," so all the "higher" forms of the mind—religion, art, philosophy—were now ousted from their superhuman position and degraded to the rank of simple "forms of social consciousness," dependent upon the material conditions of existence. Marx had "materialistically" criticized those "higher" ideological manifestations of the social consciousness even before he extended his materialistic criticism to the phenomena of the legal and political spheres. He began his attack on the existing world with a materialistic criticism of religion, art, and philosophy, and thus criticized, at first religion philosophically, and afterwards religion and philosophy politically.[3] Since he had now discovered the real basis of law and State in material production, it was only obvious that he would trace to the same real basis also those "higher" ideologies, which he had already previously traced to law and politics.

In the same way the Hegelian idea of "development" was completely "reversed" by Marx. He put in the place of the time-less development of the "idea" the real historical development of

[1] See *Encyclopædia*, § 523.
[2] See Hegel, *Philosophy of Law*, Addition to § 258.
[3] See the author's *Marxism and Philosophy*, second edition, pp. 102 *et seq.*

society on the basis of the development of its material mode of production. The Hegelian "contradiction" was replaced by the struggle of the social classes ; the dialectical "negation" by the proletariat and the dialectical "synthesis" by the proletarian revolution and the transition to a higher stage of society.

CHAPTER III

THE MATERIALISTIC SCHEME OF SOCIETY

A S early as 1843 it had become clear to Marx that Political Economy was the keystone to all social science. In the following years as a political exile in Paris and Brussels and during a first visit to London and Manchester from July to August 1845, he completed the first important portion of that Herculean task to which after a short interruption in 1848-50, he was to devote his energies throughout his life. This was not merely an investigation of particular economic topics resulting in a solution of particular economic problems. It was the initiation of a hitherto mainly politically interested philosopher into the newly discovered field of a really "materialistic" science. In the retrospective account given in the *Preface* to his *Critique of Political Economy*, 1859, he sums up the general result :

In the social production of their means of existence human beings enter into definite and necessary relations which are independent of their will—production-relations which correspond to a definite stage in the development of their material forces of production. The aggregate of these production-relations constitutes the economic structure of society, the real basis on which a juridical and political superstructure arises, and to which definite forms of social consciousness correspond. The mode of production of the material life conditions the whole process of the social, political, and intellectual life. It is not men's consciousness that determines their existence, but their social existence that determines their consciousness.

At a certain stage of their development the material productive forces of society come into contradiction with the existing production-relations, or what is only a legal expression for them with the property-relations within which they hitherto moved. From being forms of development, those

183

relations turn into fetters upon the forces of production. Then a period of social revolution sets in. With the change in the economic foundation, the whole of the vast superstructure is more or less rapidly overturned.

In considering such revolutionary processes one must always distinguish between the economic conditions of production whose material changes can be determined with the precision of natural science, and the legal, political, religious, artistic, or philosophical, in short, ideological forms in which men become conscious of this conflict and fight it out. As one cannot judge an individual by what he thinks of himself, just as little can he judge such a revolutionary epoch by its own consciousness ; he must, on the contrary, explain that consciousness by the contradictions of its material life, by the existing conflict between the social forces of production and the production-relations.

A formation of society never perishes until all the forces of production for which it is wide enough have been developed ; new and higher production-relations never come into being until the material conditions for their existence have ripened within the womb of the old society itself. Therefore mankind always sets itself such tasks only as it can solve ; for looking closer, we shall always find that the task itself arises only when the material conditions for its solution are already existent or, at least, in process of formation.

In broad outline the Asiatic, the Antique, the Feudal, and the modern Bourgeois modes of production can be designated as epochs in progress of the economic formation of society. The bourgeois production-relations are the final antagonistic form of the social production-process—antagonistic not in the sense of individual antagonism, but as growing out of the social conditions determining the life of the individuals. The forces of production developing within the womb of bourgeois society create at the same time the material conditions for the solution of that antagonism. That is why with that formation of society the pre-history of human society comes to an end.

The foregoing propositions which Marx, after fifteen years of labours presented as the carefully tested principles of his materialistic research of society, give a clear insight into the connection established by the materialistic conception of history between the social conditions of life, their historical development, and their practical overthrow.

The connection appears at first as a

static connection

linking together the different strata lying, as it were, above each other in a given socio-economico formation. That connection is alternately described as a similarity of "structure," a relation of "basis" and "superstructure," or a "correspondence" between those forms of social organization which directly spring from the process of material production and such other phenomena as arise from various other social, political and intellectual activities in any particular historical period.

This apparently static connection is, however, simply a particular case of the

dynamic connection

through which all sections and cross-sections of social life are bound together in their development. In the various phases of the origin, rise, and fall of a given socio-economic formation and its revolutionary replacement by the new and higher production-relations of a further developed social formation, that particular connection between all social conditions which, at first, from a static approach, appeared as a "consensus"[1] undergoes a change of form. From a harmonious "consensus" it is at a certain point transformed into a "dissensus." (To use the Hegelian formula: the "correspondence" already contains within itself the "contradiction" through whose further development the production-relations and, even more, the legal relations,

---

[1] It is thus described, e.g., by H. Spencer, in his *Principles of Sociology*.

forms of State, and ideologies based upon them, in due course are turned from forms of development of the forces of production into fetters restraining the further development of such forces of production.)

But this dynamic connection is not yet the final and definite form of the materialistic connection which forms the subject matter of the Marxian research. With all its apparent comprehensiveness the Marxian formula hitherto discussed in this Chapter does not aim at a complete description of the materialistic principle. It was inserted into the Preface of his main theoretical work (*Critique of Political Economy* or, as it was to be renamed later : *Capital*) for the definite purpose of disclosing to his readers the theoretical principles underlying his investigation of Political Economy as the "anatomy of bourgeois society." The historical development of society is, accordingly, represented here mainly as an objective process. History is explained as an objective development of the material forces of production at first corresponding to and then contradicting the existing production-relations, which thus from being forms of development are turned into fetters. The historical "subject" of that development is not mentioned in the formula. The production-relations of all hitherto existing economic forms of society are shown to be "antagonistic" forms of the social process of production, but the closer definition of this social antagonism as a class opposition and a class war is not given. The violent overthrow of the existing order of society by the oppressed class appears in the formula as an "epoch of social revolution" in which the superstructure of society is transformed with the change taking place in the economic foundation. And in striking contrast to the severe criticism previously raised by Marx and Engels against such a metaphysical language,[1] we read here that "mankind"

[1] See e.g., *Holy Family* (MEGA, I, iii, p. 265): "*History* does *nothing*, it possesses *no* immense wealth, it fights *no* battles ! It is rather *man*, real living *man*—who does everything, who possesses and fights; it is not History which uses men, as a means to carry out its ends as if it were a separate person, but it is *nothing* besides the activity of *man* in the pursuit of his ends."

sets itself certain tasks, and even the "epoch of transformation" itself possesses a consciousness. The aim of the whole development is not concretely defined as a transition to socialist and communist society, but is only implied in the description of present bourgeois society as being the conclusion of the "pre-history of human society."

The full sense of the materialist investigation of society results from the statements by which Marx and Engels at other times and in other contexts opposed their materialistic principle to the various conflicting opinions with which they had to deal.

The objective formula in the Preface to the *Critique of Political Economy* :

The history of society is the history of the material production and of the contradictions between the material forces of production and the production-relations which arise and are solved in the course of development

is supplemented by the subjective formula in the *Communist Manifesto* :

The history of all hitherto existing society is a history of class struggles.

The subjective formula clarifies the objective formula. It calls by its proper name the class, which brings about the objective development by a practical action. The same production-relations which fetter the forces of production (at the present stage, Capital and Wage Labour), are also the bonds of the labouring masses. The oppressed workers who in the revolutionary class struggle burst their own fetters, at the same time liberate production. The acting subject of history at the present stage is the proletariat.

Only by taking into account this

practical connection

can the theoretical statements of the materialistic investigation of society be put to their fullest use. The *theoretical fact* that

187

according to the materialistic principle of Marx legal conditions and forms of State no longer form an independent subject matter which is to be understood by virtue of its inherent qualities or derived from a higher immaterial principle but, on the contrary, are rooted in the material conditions of existing bourgeois society, coincides with the *practical fact* that in modern bourgeois society, after the abolition of all the privileges of the superior orders of the feudal society, the inequalities destroyed in the political and legal sphere are preserved in the opposition of social classes arising from the material conditions of life. By a radical elucidation of this state of affairs Marx breaks through the ideological confusion with which the panegyrists of the modern democratic State distract the attention of the proletariat from its real position, as an economically oppressed and exploited class, and from the measures to be taken for a practical change of that basic condition. Furthermore, the materialistic exposure of the illusions of the State and the law, and of all other high-pitched ideologies of modern bourgeois society, serves as a caution for the revolutionary proletarian class to keep itself free, as far as possible, from those new illusions, with which, in earlier epochs, revolutionary parties concealed from themselves the real content of the conflicts they were engaged in. For this reason Marx instilled into the minds of the workers the materialistic lesson that their emancipation from the particular form of oppression and exploitation which they suffer in the present epoch cannot result from any change of the existing political, legal, and cultural conditions, but must be brought about by themselves through a social revolution penetrating to the economic basis of existing bourgeois society.

CHAPTER IV

NATURE AND SOCIETY

MARX comprised in his materialistic investigation of society all the phenomena of a comprehensive field of experience which until then had been dealt with by a number of altogether different, old and new, sciences. On the one hand he recognized no "higher" spheres of a so-called "spiritual" life which would be exempted from the crude material necessities of the historical and social spheres. All juridical, political, religious, philosophical and artistic conceptions, the whole of the so-called "consciousness" of man and all its philosophical disguises as, for example, the Hegelian terms of an "objektiver" and "absoluter Geist," the Kantian concepts of "Gattungsvernunft," and "Bewusstsein überhaupt," the philosophical "idea" generally, and all other, even the most "universal" categories of thought exist only as given forms of a "*social consciousness,*" temporary products of a continuous development, attributes of a definite historical epoch and of a definite economic order of society. To all "legal conditions and forms of the State" there applies the materialistic principle that they can neither be understood (as the exponents of dogmatic jurisprudence and political science believe) "out of themselves" nor (as the philosophers had believed) "out of the so-called general development of the human mind," but are rooted in the material conditions of the present-day bourgeois society. To all forms of social consciousness there applies the two fold antithesis formulated by Marx in contrast both to the philosophical idealism of Kant, Fichte and Hegel, and to the naturalistic materialism of Feuerbach : "It is not the consciousness of men that determines their existence but, on

189

the contrary, their *social existence* which determines their consciousness."[1]

On the other hand, Marx comprised in his materialistic formula also the natural foundation of all historical and social phenomena and, for this purpose, conceived and represented even nature itself in the terms of a strictly historical and social science as "Industry," "Economy," or "Material Production." In spite of a genuine recognition of the "priority of external nature"[2] he does not derive the historical development of society from any kind of extra-historical and extra-social natural factors like climate, race, struggle for existence, man's physical and mental powers, etc., but from a "nature" which has itself been already "modified" by an historical and social process or, more distinctly, from the historically and socially conditioned developments of material production. The materialist philosopher Plechanov, in supporting his contrary opinion, reminds us, that "Hegel had already noted in his *Philosophy of History* the important part played by the geographical foundations of the world history."[3] He did not see that the scientific advances made by Marx's historical and social materialism over the idealism of Hegel and the materialism of Feuerbach consists just in this difference that he conceived of "matter" itself in historical terms, while all his philosophical predecessors, both the idealistic and the materialistic brand had conceived of "matter" as a dumb, dead or, at the utmost, biologically animated nature only.

While according to Hegel "physical nature, indeed, exerts a direct effect upon world history,"[4] Marx started from an altogether different viewpoint from the outset. Physical nature

[1] The words emphasized above show the difference between the social approach of Marx and the naturalistic formula contained in Feuerbach *Preliminary Theses for the Reform of Philosophy*, 1842: "Thought comes from being, but being does not come from thought."
[2] See MEGA, I, v, p. 33.
[3] See Plechanov, *The Fundamental Problems of Marxism*, VI.
[4] See Hegel, *Philosophy of History*, General Introduction, II, i (a); and *Special Introduction*, II, "*The natural connection or the geographical basis of world history*."

according to him, does not directly enter into history. It does so by indirection, i.e., as a process of material production which goes on not only between man and nature, but at the same time between man and men.[1] Or, to use a phraseology which will be clear even to the philosophers, in the strictly social research of Marxian materialism that "pure" nature which is presupposed to all human activity (the economic *natura naturans*) is replaced everywhere by a "nature" mediated and modified through human social activity, and thus at the same time capable of a further change and modification by our own present and future activity, i.e., by nature as *material production* (or the economic *natura naturata*).[2]

Being "social," nature has a specifically historical character varying in the different epochs. As an historical and social nature it has above all, a distinct class character. For example, as emphasized by Marx in his controversy with Feuerbach, that cherry tree before the philosopher's window, whose ancestors were "artificially" transplanted to Europe a few hundred years ago, is thereby for the modern European no nature-given growth ;[3] just as, on the same grounds, the potato is no "nature-given" food for the modern European poor, or, at most, only in the same sense as the adulterated bread and the "sophisticated" wine sold in the back streets are "nature-given" products of the modern capitalist mode of production.[4] The den of the modern poor is even less than the lair of the wild beast a "nature-given" shelter in which he can move at ease like the fish in the water. It is not a house where he can feel at home, but it is the house of his landlord who will evict him when he cannot afford to pay his rent.[5] "My house is my castle" originating from the world

[1] See *Holy Family* (MEGA, I, iii, p. 19), and *Wage-Labour and Capital* (MEGA, I, vi, pp. 482 *et seq.*).
[2] See for a more detailed discussion, Marx's *Economico-philosophical MSS. of 1844* (MEGA, I, iii, p. 121-23) and *German Ideology* (MEGA I, v, pp. 10-11, 32 *et seq.*).
[3] See MEGA), I, v, pp. 32-33.
[4] See *Capital*, I, pp. 137, 210-13, 565.
[5] See MEGA, I, iii, pp. 135-36.

of simple commodity production, holds good for the slum barracks of our big cities no more than it did for the cots of the English farm-labourers of 1860, as described in *Capital*.[1] Modern "hunger," which satisfies itself with cooked meat, eaten with knife and fork, is quite another thing than that hunger which "swallowed raw meat with the aid of hand, nail and tooth."[2] So do those "normal" periods of hunger natural to primitive hordes, that have been artificially reintroduced in modern capitalist society for those sections of the unemployed who, for some reason or another, have been taken off the dole, represent a vastly different thing from the hunger, be it ever so great, that may occasionally, by the accident of a temporary stoppage of their regular food supplies, cause a "thrilling" sensation to the idle rich.

None of those things, in the definite forms, in which they appear in present bourgeois society or for that matter in any earlier or later epochs, comes from "nature" alone. They depend upon the existing historical conditions of material production and can be changed with the change of those conditions. This happens through an historical development, which may take a shorter or longer time, but which is nowhere stopped by any absolute barrier, through an objective process which is at the same time a struggle between social classes.

This viewpoint of a strictly *social*, that is of an *historical* and *practical* science dominated from the very beginning the whole novel system of concepts which Marx and Engels built up in their controversy with the then existing idealistic and materialistic currents of thought. The existence of physical man, the external world in which he moves, and the natural objective development of those natural conditions in large periods of "cosmological time," independent of that altogether different development of the social forms which is accomplished by man's action in "historical time," all these "real presuppositions" of

[1] See *Capital*, I, pp. 648-658.   [2] See *Introduction*, 1857, p. 717.

history and society are, of course, real presuppositions also for the materialistic research of Marx. They do not, however, appear as theoretical premises within the system of the new social science which starts from its own materialistic principles defined in historical and social terms.

This is no way contradicted but, on the contrary, even more clearly demonstrated by the terms of so-called *"naturally grown forms of society"* and of so-called *"social laws of nature"* which are continually used by Marx in the presentation of his theory. The concept of *"natural growth"* as applied to historical forms, has with Marx an altogether different meaning than it had with the historians, poets, and philosophers of the "Romanticist School" who in a conscious opposition to the preceding period of Enlightenment and Revolution glorified everything "naturally grown." Marx, on the contrary, used the term in a negative sense for the description of such conditions, relations, connections which have not as yet been subjected to a conscious human action. In this sense Marx speaks in his Critique of the *German Ideology* and twenty years later, in *Capital*, of the "nature-grown" ("naturwuechsige") forms of division of labour,[1] of a world-wide historical connection between individuals,[2] of the State,[3] of legal conditions,[4] of language,[5] and of such apparently immutable differences as the variations of race.[6] In all these cases the "naturwüchsige" form of a social relation is in contrast to those other forms which this relation assumes in the course of social development when it is either consciously maintained and further worked out, or changed to a greater or lesser extent by a conscious human action. The "naturwuechsige" forms are thus described as social forms which have arisen historically just as all other, more or less consciously created forms and are therefore capable of a further change both in the present and the

[1] See MEGA, I, v, pp. 12, 20-22, 41-42, 49-50, 55 *et seq.*, and *Capital*, I pp. 316, 321, 329, etc.
[2] See MEGA, I, v, pp. 26-7.   [3] *Ibid.* p. 325.   [4] *Ibid.* p. 342.
[5] *Ibid.* pp. 404-405.   [6] *Ibid.* p. 403.

future. Thus they are not eternal forms of all social life but can be overthrown by the united individuals in a deliberate action, which will finally strip them of their present crude and oppressive "nature-grown" character. One sees at first glance the positive bearing of this thought not only on the theoretical extension of the realm of social knowledge but also on the practical socialistic and communistic tendencies which are necessarily bound up with this knowledge.[1]

The same holds good for the other apparently nature-bound term of the new Marxian science, which we have already discussed when dealing with the economic law of value, i.e., the so-called "*social laws of nature.*" Here again we have to deal with a term which is at first defined in a negative manner only.[2] The economic laws prevailing in the capitalistic mode of production do not have within the new materialistic science of society that positive and final meaning which the real "laws of nature" have for the physicist[3] and which, according to their first discoverers and inventors, pertained also to those "natural" laws which would in future govern the new "civil" mode of existence emerging from the artificial fetters of mediæval feudalism. They are even less what Marx and Engels in their earlier, philosophical, period called a "law of the mind" as opposed to a "mere law of nature"[4] and what recurs in their later writings when they speak of a "leap from the realm of necessity into the realm of freedom"[5] and of the "true realm of freedom blossoming out of the realm of necessity in the fully developed Communist Society of the future."[6]

[1] See MEGA, I, v, p. 60.
[2] See the definition given by Engels in his *Outlines of a Critique of National Economy*, 1844 (MEGA, I, ii, p. 394) and quoted with approval by Marx in *Capital*, I, pp. 41-42, footnote 28: "What are we to think of a law that can only establish itself through periodical revolutions? Well, it is a law of nature resulting from the unconsciousness of the people concerned."
[3] See Marx's letter to Kugelmann of 11.7.1868.
[4] See Engels, l.c.
[5] See Engels, *Anti-Dühring*, 1878.
[6] See Marx, *Capital*, III, ii, p. 355.

However, just from the negative definition that the so-called "laws of nature" of the bourgeois economists are, in fact, not laws of nature at all, there derives the positive significance which the term of the "social" laws of nature assumes in the revolutionary science of Marx. The fact that the general conditions of bourgeois society which had been proclaimed as laws by the bourgeois economists, are restricted to a definite historical epoch, implies that in the further development of society all those apparent laws can be abrogated through the conscious social act of the class which is at present oppressed by them, to be replaced by another, a willed and planned form of the social activities of man.

Thus neither of the two Marxian terms conforms with the perpetuation of the so-called economic laws asserted by the classical economists ; even less with that further extension of the realm of "natural growth in society" which had been the dream of the early counter-revolutionary theorists in France and of the German and English romanticists. Marx, on the contrary, applies both terms for the purpose of extending the realm of history and society, i.e., of a conscious social action as against the so-called eternal necessities of an altogether inaccessible "realm of nature." Far behind the "immutable laws" invented and maintained by the bourgeois economists for the preservation of an order of production allegedly "natural" and "rational," but in fact ever more artificial, more arbitrary, and ever more dependent on force, and at the same time more hampering to the further development of society and more destructive of human life, stand those real necessities of nature which condition the whole life of man and which are also recognized by the Marxists as unchangeable facts and as natural presuppositions of all social development. Even this recognition applies to a given time only. There is, from the historical and social principle of Marxian science, no absolute and predetermined limit beyond which an apparently "naturwüchsige" foundation of all social life might not in future be discovered to be no more than an historical and historically changeable form, and thus a form which can be modified and overthrown by a conscious action. "Even the naturally-grown variations of the human species such as differences of race, etc., can and must be abolished in the historical process."[1]

As with all other innovations embodied in the new materialistic theory, Marx's methodical extension of society at the expense of nature is proved mainly on the field of economic science. The Marxian critique of the fetish character of the commodity and of all other economic categories refutes once and for all those mystical ideas by which the earlier economists had attributed economic phenomena to an immediate physical cause, be it some external force of nature, or the physical constitution of man or, finally, his so-called "innate" psychological qualities. There is, above all, no such thing as an immediate "natural basis of the surplus value." The only significance which can be claimed for physical conditions in the genesis of the socio-historical phenomenon of the exploitation of property-less wage-labourers by property-owning capitalists, is that of a natural limit or barrier fixing the points at which the labour-time necessary for the maintenance and reproduction of the labourer ceases and thus "labour for others can begin." *"In proportion as industry advances, those natural limits recede."*[2]

The same applies to the so-called "natural basis of the State" which is asserted by a whole school of modern bourgeois sociologists. The political phenomenon of the State results, in fact, as little from unchangeable physical conditions as the economic phenomenon of the surplus value upon which it depends as a secondary and derived form. Just as things useful for human needs and produced by human labour are "commodities," and gold and silver are "money," under definite social conditions only and not by any inherent physical qualities,

[1] See MEGA, I, v, p. 403.   [2] See *Capital*, I, pp. 475-479.

so is the physically weaker individual or race the slave of the physically stronger not by any eternal necessity but through the accident of temporary circumstances. By a definite historical process the class which under the social conditions prevailing in the present epoch produces all social wealth, has been separated from the material means of production and is now ruled and exploited by the class which through the same historical process has monopolized for itself the means of social production as "capital." The apparently "naturalistic" theory which assigns such existing social and political facts to the Command of Nature is but a secularized form of those older theories which derived the same facts from the Command of God or, for that matter, from such intermediate agencies as the philosophical unfolding of an eternal Idea, Reason, or Humanity itself.

CHAPTER V

PRODUCTIVE FORCES AND PRODUCTION-RELATIONS

THE driving forces of the revolutionary development of society, according to Marx, are the potential powers of production inherent in a given epoch of the socio-economic formation. Like all other terms of the new social science, the concept of the "productive forces" is defined by Marx not a priori but empirically. It is described in terms of economics and history and in reference to a specific mode of production, not in terms of a general sociology ; not dogmatically, but critically ; not from the view-point of a pre-established harmony, but from that of class opposition ; not for the purpose of theoretical knowledge and contemplation, but with a view to social action or "revolutionary practice." Thus the productive forces as conceived by Marx are much more than a mere philosophical concept of "matter" resulting from the "materialistic reversal" of the Hegelian "idea" and, like its predecessor, presupposed to all empirical knowledge. They form, together with the "production-relations" in which they function and develop, the real whole of the given "mode of material production" which can be determined "with the precision of a natural science."

There is in this Marxian term nothing mystical and nothing metaphysical. A "productive force" is, at first, nothing else than the real labour power of working men ; the force incorporated in these living human beings by which, with definite material means of production and within a definite form of social co-operation conditioned by those material means of production, they produce through their labour the material means of satisfying the social needs of their existence, that is—under capitalistic conditions, "commodities." In a second and even more important sense, everything that increases the productive effect of the human labour power (and thereby, under capitalistic conditions, inevitably increases at the same time the profit of its exploiters) is said by Marx to be a "productive force." To the productive forces in that dynamic sense belongs the progress of technique and science ; there belongs above all the social organization itself or the immediately "social" forces created by co-operation and division of labour. In this sense, Adam Smith had emphasized in his economic work the *"proportionable increase of the productive powers of labour"* occasioned by the division of labour under the conditions of modern industry,[1] and we may say without exaggeration that the basic term of Marx's revolutionary theory, the concept of the "social" productive forces, originated just from that Smithian thought[2] though the implications of the new term were but partially and one-sidedly described by Smith and were brought out in their full economic and social significance only by the new materialistic theory of the proletarian revolution.

"The production of the human life," as stated by Marx in an early exposition of his new principle, "appears from the outset as a two-fold relation. It is, on the one hand, a natural relation and on the other hand a social relation, social in the sense of a co-operation between several individuals no matter under what conditions, in what way, and for what purpose. It follows that a definite mode of production or industrial stage always concurs with a definite mode of co-operation or social stage, and *this mode of co-operation is itself a productive force*."[3] So does the real point in all later developments of the revolutionary theory of Marx consist in the emphasis laid on that "*new potential of productive force*" which, increasing continually in the course of the development of human society, inexhaustibly flows from

[1] See Adam Smith, *The Wealth of Nations*, I, i.
[2] See Marx's extracts from Smith on first reading his work in the unpublished *Notes of 1844* (MEGA, I, iii, pp. 457 *et seq.*).
[3] See Marx, *German Ideology*, 1845-46 (MEGA, I, v, p. 19).

the many single forces melted together into one united force. Under capitalistic conditions this new force seems to spring from the productivity of "capital." In truth it springs from the growing productivity of social labour.[1]

From this derives a third and final sense in which the Marxian term is applied to the workers themselves who by a revolutionary action as a class set free the forces potentially existing in social labour to-day. That potential power will be fully actualized by the proletarian revolution which will break the restraints put on the productivity of society by the present capitalistic form of commodity production and unite the hitherto incompletely co-ordinated forces of the single labourers into an organized collective labour force. It is partially realized to-day wherever in the various forms of the proletarian class struggle, the strike, the stay-in strike, and the general strike, the united workers stand up against the oppressive forces of capital. Thus it may be said that under the present conditions of an ever-increasing sabotage of the powerful capacities of modern industry by the existing capitalistic production-relations the new potential of productivity inherent in the working class reveals itself most clearly in those cases when, according to the isolating and static concepts of the bourgeois ideologists the labourers cease to function as a "productive force" at all, but in fact only cease to function as a "productive force of capital" and stand ready to realize that incomparably greater power of productivity which is potentially existent in the material means of production and in the hands and brains of the toiling masses to-day. *"De tous les instruments de production, le plus grand pouvoir productif, c'est la classe révolutionnaire elle-même."*[2]

It follows from the foregoing discussion that those recent Marx interpreters are quite mistaken who, by a direct inversion

[1] See Marx, *Wage-Labour and Capital*, (MEGA, I, vi, pp. 482 *et seq.*) and, for an exhaustive discussion of this point, *Capital*, I, xi, under the heading *Co-operation*.
[2] See Marx, *Anti-Proudhon*, 1847 (MEGA, I, vi, p. 227).

of the order in which theory and practice were blended by Marx into a dynamic whole, wanted to degrade the opposition between the social classes to a temporary appearance of the underlying "economic" contradiction between the productive forces and production-relations as a larger and assumedly more "material" entity. They inflate the scientific principle of Marx's economic research to a universal and eternal Dialectic pervading the whole development of nature and man and thus fall back not only far behind historical materialism, but behind the historical idealism of Hegel and his equally idealistic philosophical predecessors.[1]

On the other hand, the Marxian "contradiction of productive forces and production-relations" means much more than a lack of adjustment between technical results and their social application. The Marxian concept of "social" productive forces has nothing in common with the idealistic abstractions of the old and new "Technocrats" who imagine that they can define and measure the productive powers of society apart from all social conditions in terms of natural science and technology. There is no doubt that the productive forces include, along with the social nature of the labour engaged in material production, also the "improvements on the field of intellectual production, especially in natural science and its practical application."[2] The "fettering character" of the existing capitalistic production-relations appears also in the frustration of intellectual labour, which results from the fact that the ruling class of present capitalistic society is interested in technical progress only indirectly, i.e., only in so far as it can thereby increase its profits. A scientific investigation into the definite forms of the growing repression of technical progress by the so-called necessities of the capitalistic production is a powerful indictment against the existing capitalistic system. But the conflict of technical and social possibilities is by no means the only form in which the struggle

[1] See the author's contribution to the Symposium "Why I am a Marxist?" in *Modern Monthly*, April, 1935.
[2] See Marx, *Capital*, I, pp. 350-51, and III, i, pp. 55-56.

between the progressive tendency of the material productive forces and the stagnation resulting from the fixed form of the social relations of production manifests itself in present society. Technical knowledge and "technocratic" prescriptions are not sufficient in themselves to remove the material obstacles which oppose any important change in present-day capitalistic society, and these can, indeed, not be removed by intellectual weapons alone. There is more power of resistance in the mute force of economic conditions and in the economically and politically organized forces of the class interested in the maintenance of those conditions than well-meaning technocrats have ever dreamt of. "Technocracy," said Trotzky in a bold forecast of *The Future of Socialism in America*,[1] "can only be realized in a soviet régime when the barriers of private property have fallen."

Even before Marx had discovered in the so-called "economic law" of the *accumulation of capital* the ultimate material reason of the characteristic historical fact that capitalistic production cannot exist without a continuous progress,[2] he had been aware of this fundamental law of modern society. The revolutionary role of the bourgeoisie determined by it is described in the *Communist Manifesto* :

The bourgeoisie cannot exist without constantly revolutionizing the instruments of production, and thereby the relations of production, and with them the whole relations of society. Conservation of the old modes of production in unaltered form was, on the contrary, the first condition of existence for all earlier industrial classes. A constant overthrow of production, uninterrupted disturbance of all social conditions, everlasting uncertainty and agitation distinguish the bourgeois from all earlier epochs. All stable, rust-fixed relations, with their train of ancient and venerable views and opinions, are swept away, those which are newly formed,

---

[1] See Trotzky in *Die Sammlung*, June 1935, p. 522.
[2] See *Capital*, I, xxi *et seq.*, especially pp. 587 *et seq.* The theory of accumulation is further developed in *Capital*, II, Part III.

become antiquated before they can ossify. All that is established and has a status, evaporates, all that is holy is profaned, and man is at last compelled to face with sober senses his real position in life and his actual conditions.

In the first ascending phase of the bourgeois epoch this law of a society based on the capitalistic mode of production was naively and candidly formulated by its ideological supporters as a "law of progress."[1] When afterwards, especially since Darwin, the simple concept of "progress" was supplanted by the more elaborate concept of "evolution" that change resulted at first only in a further development and wider application of the same fundamental principle. The concept of a permanent "progressive evolution" was raised to a fundamental principle of sociological science. In this sense, Herbert Spencer endeavoured to represent the study of sociology as "the study of Evolution in its most complex form."[2]

Later bourgeois sociology from the standpoint of its higher learning smiled at the unsophisticated belief in progress which had been characteristic of its own beginnings. Spencer himself although still adhering to the idea of a general progress involving as its inevitable consequence a higher moral development, formulated at the same time the far more neutral definition of development as "a progress from a simple to a complex form."[3] Huxley emphasized the ethical indifference of the idea of evolution by pointing to the lack of a necessary connection, and even partial contradiction, between socio-economic and ethical progress.[4] That "pluralist" approach was during the further development of bourgeois sociology transformed into a

[1] See Perrault, *Paralèlle des anciens et des modernes*, 1688-97. For a modern discussion of the question first raised in that book, see G. Sorel, *Les illusions du progrès*, 1908.
[2] See Spencer, *Study of Sociology*, 1874, pp. 384-85, see also M. Ginsberg, The Concept of Evolution in *"Studies of Sociology,"* 1932, and J. Rumney, *Herbert Spencer's Sociology*, 1934.
[3] See Rumney, l.c. ; especially pp. 242 *et seq.*, and pp. 272 *et seq.*
[4] See T. H. Huxley, *Evolution and Ethics*, 1893, pp. 31 *et seq.*

KARL MARX

complete scepticism of progress, and finally into social pessimism, glorification of reaction and *"Decline of the West."*

As the original idea of progress expressed the ascendant phase of capitalist production, its declining phase is manifested in the gradual transformation of that idea into the "neutral" and "non-evaluative" concept of development current among the modern bourgeois sociologists. With the further development of capitalistic production, with the increase of accumulated capital and wealth, the capitalist ceased to be a mere incarnation of that uninterrupted and uninterruptedly accelerated accumulation of capital which in the earlier phase had been reflected as a "fanaticism of progress" in the social consciousness of the time. A long hangover followed upon the previous state of rapture and intoxication with progress.

The idea of progress abandoned by bourgeois science was kept alive by the class which represented the progressive tendency within the practical development of the new epoch. The criticism directed by the Utopian socialism of St. Simon and Fourier and by the materialistic communism of Owen and Marx against the bourgeois concept of "progress" is, in part, a restoration and further development of the rational kernel of that same early bourgeois idea. Socialism achieves in a changed form and in an enormously increased measure once more that unfettering of the material forces of production which capitalism had endeavoured to achieve in a form adapted to the time and in which ultimately it had more or less failed. The working class must adhere to the bourgeois principle of progress through all the phases of the long struggle in which it is still striving to work out its own emancipation and with it a new and higher form of society. Not until that phase of the communist society of the future, when the enslaving subordination of man under the existing system of division of labour and the resulting antagonism between intellectual and physical labour will have been finally conquered ; when labour will have developed from being

204

a means of living to a spontaneous activity of man and, along with a development of all creative powers of the human individual the productive forces of society will also have increased ; not till all springs of co-operative wealth are in full flow—not until then will the inhuman sacrifice of the present for the future of society become superfluous and the single-track idea of "progress" branch out into the *universal development of free individuals in a free society*.[1] Not till then will the modern working class, by its conscious action, realize the old dream of the oppressed classes of all times which already in Aristotle[2] had been a mythical expression for the real goal of the revolutionary self-emancipation of the helot class.

Until then the proletariat reproaches the ruling classes much less for realizing the productive forces only in a capitalist fashion and thus burdening the working class with the enormous costs and sufferings of this capitalistic form of progress than it reproaches them for carrying out that progress less and less efficiently, for adhering, in an ever increasing degree, to their own narrow class interests which become more and more irreconcilable with the further development of the social productive powers, and, for a direct and conscious sabotage of every social progress. The first result of the proletarian class-struggle is to force upon the bourgeoisie, against its own will, the continuation of its historical vocation as a capitalistic class.

Long before the proletariat will overthrow the ruling bourgeoisie, and constitute itself a ruling class and the official bearer of social development, it does anticipate this great change by its own development into an independent revolutionary class, by the gradual growth of its class consciousness and by the multiple forms of a veritable class war waged against the existing capitalistic

[1] See Marx, *Marginal Notes to the Programme of the German Labour Party*, 1875 (*Neue Zeit*, IX, i, 1891, pp. 563-75) and the concluding sentence of the second section of the *Communist Manifesto*, on the ultimate goal of an "association in which the free development of each member is the condition for the free development of all" (MEGA, I, vi, p. 546).

[2] Aristotle, *Politics*, I, iv.

production-relations and their political superstructure. Even the progress thus imposed upon the bourgeoisie is, from the viewpoint of the proletariat, no longer a bourgeois progress, but the workers' own affair. The progressive development of the social productive forces becomes the action of the proletarian class.[1]

The bourgeoisie had become conscious of the economic law of its own development in a mystified form only ; it had expended the accumulation of capital into ⌐ cosmic law of progress. The proletariat puts in place of that ideological mystification, a clear and scientific orientation of its own social theory and practice to a further progressive development of the hitherto evolved productive forces.

In order to fulfil that progressive task, the proletariat will first find it necessary to tear asunder in a social revolution those strongest fetters of the productive forces which are formed by the capitalistic mode of production. "*The real historical barrier of capitalistic production is capital itself.*"[2]

Even the bourgeois revolution of the preceding epoch which was described one-sidedly by its ideological supporters as a change of civil constitution, the laws, and the State, in short, as a "political" revolution only, was in fact an overthrow of the whole socio-economic formation. The historical blindness of the bourgeois revolutionaries which persists in the bourgeois conception of the revolutionary process to-day lies, above all, in the fact that they considered the change in the economic conditions of life not yet as a direct task, but as a "natural" consequence resulting, as it were, spontaneously from the essential achievement of the political revolution.

The proletarian criticism of the traditional bourgeois concepts of progress, evolution, and of a merely political revolution, is

---

[1] See *Anti-Proudhon*, ii, § 5 (MEGA, I, vi, pp. 221-28) and *Communist Manifesto* (MEGA, I, vi, pp. 533-37). See also the author's *Law of Labour*, Berlin 1922, pp. 46 *et seq.*
[2] See *Capital*, III, p. 231.

based on the materialistic discovery that the social "production-relations" corresponding to each stage of the development of the material productive forces do not develop either in an independent economic "evolution" or as a "natural result" of a merely political revolution. They have to be changed by man. Nay more, the new political and ideological conditions temporarily achieved by a mere political revolution can only be upheld against the powers of reaction by a radical social revolution reaching down to the very roots of the existing order of society, that is, right down to material production.

The only "evolution" that is possible and actually takes place within the framework of the existing production-relations of an historical epoch, i.e., the only process of development which leaves the basic structure of a given society "on the whole" or "essentially" unchanged is the intrinsic development of the social "productive forces." The material conditions of the new and higher production-relations which are to be substituted for the existing production-relations by a social revolution are brought to maturity within the womb of the old society. Thus the production-relations, unable to develop by themselves, nevertheless fulfil for a certain time and up to a certain point a positive function on the development of material production. Within them there proceeds the further development of the old, and the growth of the new productive forces.

The latent, potential, dynamic further development of material production going on within a fundamentally unchanged system of production-relations occupies the first phase of every historical epoch. As soon as the harmonious development, or rather an externally "harmonious" development only, which contains the hidden germs of a future conflict, has reached a certain point, it loses even that outwardly harmonious aspect. "At a certain stage of their development," said Marx, "the material productive forces of society come into contradiction with the existing production-relations within which they hitherto moved.

207

From being forms of development they turn into fetters of the productive forces. Then an epoch of social revolution sets in. With the change in the economic foundation the whole of the vast superstructure is more or less rapidly overturned."[1]

This dynamic conception of *material production* itself, distinguishes the Marxian theory of the social revolution from all other revolutionary theories. Although revelling in "dynamics" and "development," the bourgeois sociologists remain the slaves of a fundamentally "static" concept at the most important point ; they are not able to extend their "dynamic" terms to the very foundation of society. The material mode of production in a given epoch of society forms for them a closed system which is determined throughout. In it production is carried on in definite forms. The whole of the existing productive forces of society is actualized in these forms. There is no room in this conception for any surplus or unutilized fund of productive powers that might possibly be added to those really active productive powers. They take seriously what was presented as a terrific indictment against the existing capitalistic system by the late German socialist leader, August Bebel ; "Without profits, no chimney smokes." According to this view, the capitalistic production-relations together with the corresponding relations of distribution are just as indispensable for the productive process as is the land, the raw materials, machines, and labouring "hands." From this static viewpoint it amounts almost to a miracle that production has been able to develop at all and thus to get from its past to its present stage. This miracle is either explained by a pseudo-scientific disintegration of real change into smaller and smaller steps of a gradual and imperceptible evolution,[2] or else it is disposed of by reference to the supernatural creative forces

[1] See *Preface* 1859.
[2] This logical fallacy was critically exposed by Hegel in his *Science of Logic*, I, pp. 383-84. Marx illustrated the equation between a real change and an infinity of alterations "so minute that they can be ignored" by a reference to the foolish maid who excused her mistake by saying that "the baby was at first so very little."

of the "great bourgeois revolution" of the past which exploded once for all the obsolete feudal order that was in itself no longer capable of any further development and created the modern industrial system capable of an unlimited evolution.

The apparently undivided whole of a given material production is split by Marx into fixed production-relations and elastic productive forces. Thus material production is stripped of its closed character, its immovability, and unchangeability. The production-relations are now no longer asked whether production can go on within them. They are asked, above all, whether a further development of production can go on within them. They are the forms that either advance or block the development of the productive forces. Conversely, the existence and extent of the potential productive forces inherent in the present mode of production cannot be tested by a technological calculation so long as they cannot be tested in their actual working within a given social process of production, and as the way for the real test has not been cleared by the revolutionary destruction of the capitalistic barrier. Like the mutations of animals and plants which have replaced the older evolutionary concepts in modern biology, the "*social mutations*" occurring in the material mode of production[1] are not completely determined and determinable in advance. Just as the mutation is a "leap of nature," in spite of Aristotle, so is the social revolution in its actual process, with all materialistic determination of its premises and forms, a "leap," not from an absolute "realm of necessity" into an absolute "realm of freedom," but from a rigid system of long-established and repressive social relations to a flexible system of new and more plastic forms of social life as yet in the

[1] The term "mutation" which to-day is mainly used in natural science was first applied to those historical and social events which to day would be called a revolution. The term "revolution" was only recently transferred from the field where it was most impressively used by Copernicus in 1543, to its present principal application. It was not applied in this sense until the end of the 17th century and obtained its full present significance with the French revolution of 1789.

process of formation, with plenty of room for a further development of the productive forces and for new forms of human activity.[1]

The social revolution of the proletariat is an action of men united in a definite social class and engaged in a war against other social classes, with all the chances and all the risks attached to such a real practical effort. This is in no way contradicted by the Marxian statement of 1859 that "a formation of society never perishes before all the forces of production for which it is wide enough have developed"; and that "new and higher production-relations never come into being before the material conditions for their existence have matured within the womb of the old society itself." There is no reason to suspect, as some bourgeois and reformist opponents of Marx's revolutionary theory have done, that Marx had by this time abandoned the practical materialistic standpoint of his earlier writings (Theses on Feuerbach, German Ideology, Misère de la philosophie, and Communist Manifesto) and had adopted a "fatalistic" conception of the revolutionary process as a purely economic development brought about by the working of an inevitable law. Marx had formed his materialistic opinion that "l'organisation des éléments révolutionnaires comme classe suppose l'existence de toutes les forces productives qui pouvaient s'engendrer dans le sein de la société ancienne," long before the failure of the bourgeois revolution of 1848 and the ensuing reaction and despair could have turned him from a "militant propagandist of the revolutionary class struggle" into a "detached scientific observer of the real historical development." Such difference as there is between the earlier and later formulations of the materialistic principle, consists in a shift of emphasis from the subjective factor of revolutionary class war to its connection with the underlying objective development. This shift of emphasis appears for the

[1] See the sentences quoted above, p. 94, from Engels, *Anti-Düehing*, and from Marx, *Capital*, III. See further *Communist Manifesto*, 1848, and Marx, *Marginal Notes to the Programme of the German Labour Party*, 1875.

first time in a document of the autumn of 1850 in which Marx and Engels drew attention to the restored prosperity and the consequent temporary close of the revolutionary movement. "Under the conditions of this general prosperity, when the productive forces of bourgeois society develop as abundantly as is at all possible within existing bourgeois conditions, there can be no question of a real revolution. Such a revolution is only possible in those periods when the two factors, the modern productive forces and the bourgeois forms of production, come to contradict one another."[1] By this sober, materialistic state-ment they disowned "the illusions of the vulgar democracy grouped around the would-be provisional governments in partibus"[2] and thus separated themselves once for all from the leaders of the revolutionary bourgeois emigration of 1848 "who later, almost without exception, have made their peace with Bismarck—so far as Bismarck found them worth the trouble."[3] More important, by the same act they broke with the so-called "partisans of action" who at that time under the leadership of Willich and Schapper had swept with their illusionary hopes of a speedy new outbreak of the defeated revolutionary movement the majority of the reconstituted Communist League of 1850. So bitter was the ensuing fight that it led to a formal split within the then most advanced proletarian party[4] and to an eventual dissolution of the whole orgainzation.

As we have seen in discussiing the successive phases of Marx's economic theory[5] the new form of Marx's revolutionary

---

[1] See *Neue Rheinische Zeitung, politisch-oekonomische Revue*, No. 5-6, Hamburg 1850.
[2] See Engels, Introduction to his 1895 edition of the articles contributed by Marx and himself to *Neue Rheinische Zeitung, politisoh oekonomische Revue* (reprinted in that edition under the title *Class Struggles in France*, 1850-50).
[3] *Ibid.*
[4] See the reasons offered by Marx for his motion as embodied in the record of the proceedings of the last meeting of the London Central Executive Committee of the Communist League, 15.9.1850, later published by Marx in his *Disclosures on the Communist Trial at Cologne*, 1852.
[5] See above, pp. 110 *et seq.*

materialism was due to the changed conditions which were henceforth given for the practical development of the proletarian class struggle. The stronger emphasis now laid on the objective presuppositions of a victorious proletarian revolution which cannot be replaced by good will, by the right theory, or by the most efficient organization of the revolutionaries, appears from this point of view in the main as a lesson drawn from the experiences of the European revolution and counter-revolution of 1848 for the benefit of the new phase of the revolutionary labour movement which began in 1850. In a similar manner, the revolutionary Marxist, Lenin, on a closely analagous occasion, summed up for the benefit of the Russian and international militant party the tactical experiences of the three Russian revolutions of the 20th century. In what he now called the "fundamental law of revolution," he stated the indispensable objective conditions of a "direct, open, really revolutionary struggle of the working class." Just as Marx and Engels, after the final defeat of the 1848 revolution, had confronted the subjective and emotional hopes of the Leftists of 1850 with the cruel materialistic analysis of the objective economic position and the sober perspective resulting therefrom, so Lenin came to grips with the activistic revolutionary tendencies of the left communists of 1920 who in an objectively changed situation adhered to the slogans of the direct revolutionary situation released by the Great War.[1] While thus warning the vanguard of the working class not to stick too conservatively to the direct revolutionary tactics which were no longer justified by objective conditions, both Marx and Lenin did not think for a moment of supplanting the real revolutionary action of the working class by a passive belief in a mere economic process of development which would after a considerable amount of waiting finally achieve the revolutionary change with the inevitability of a

[1] See Lenin, *Radicalism, an Infantile Disease of Communism*, written 27.4.1920—12.5.1920.

natural process. The class which stands in the midstream of historical development and by its own movement determines that development, must by its conscious activity finally prove the maturity reached by the productive forces within the existing production-relations. They must with their own hands break the fetters that obstruct the development of the productive forces and establish the higher production-relations of a new progressive epoch of society.

CHAPTER VI

BASIS AND SUPERSTRUCTURE

WHAT are the particular relations between the "economic structure of society" and its political and juridical "superstructure," between "social existence" and "social consciousness ?" In what definite forms is the material connection between the various fields of social life realized ? What is their significance for a materialistic investigation of the different spheres of a given economic order of society ?

We know already that all these apparently separated and widely different spheres form together a universe of society in which, just as in a living organism, every part is connected with every other part. This "just as," by the way, is to be read as meaning "just as much and just as *little*." The author does not want in either case to be regarded as adhering to that mystic and unscientific theory of "whole-ism" according to which this connection is previously granted and needs only to be discovered in detail by the endeavours of the investigator. He would rather, with old Kant, regard the idea of whole-ism as a working principle which guides our strictly empirical research and may or may not hold good even in a given instance. The position to-day is different from that which prevailed at the time when Marx had first to establish the materialistic principle against a host of deep-rooted idealistic prejudices. Marx himself nowhere discussed the question in a general way.[1] But it follows from his criticism of the equally metaphysical bourgeois concept of Evolution,[2] from the principles of specification and change

---

[1] For a discussion of Marx's attitude towards the "whole-ism" of Hegel see Rebecca Cooper, *The Logical Influence of Hegel on Marx*, Seattle, 1925, pp. 178 *et seq.*, and Sidney Hook, *From Hegel to Marx*, London, New York, 1936, pp. 62 *et seq.*

[2] See above, pp. 51 *et seq.*

underlying his whole work and, even more, from the methods actually applied by him in the investigation of the economic sphere in *Capital*, that he would have ruled out the words "all" and "every" just as well from that broader universe of a strictly empirical and critical research which he called alternately "history" or "society" or the realm of "practical action." He would have replaced those vague and meaningless generalities by a specific description of a given state of society, its historical genesis, and its inherent developmental tendencies from the practical viewpoint of the working class.

Marx had not passed in vain through the school of Hegel which had been for the whole generation of the revolutionaries of the 30's and 40's the great school of philosophical thought. He brought to his materialistic research a method of inquiry ranging from the most exact theoretical to the most direct practical knowledge. Unfortunately, that broadness and subtlety of Marx's thought has been less and less understood by its later exponents and opponents. Thus one group fell into the error that, according to the materialistic theory, a full material reality pertained only to the economic phenomena, while all other social phenoma—State, law, forms of consciousness possessed a lesser and lesser degree of "reality" and ultimately were lost in pure "ideology."[1] According to this first misconception which will hereafter be called the "economistic" tendency, it is only the economic struggle of the workers and the forms of social struggle springing directly from it which are recognized as a direct proletarian and revolutionary action, whereas all other forms of struggle, and more especially "political action," are regarded as an undesirable deviation from the real revolutionary aims. This economistic tendency was represented during Marx's lifetime, within the Working Men's International Organization, by the adherents of Proudhon, by Bakunin, and other

---

[1] For a more detailed discussion see the author's *Marxism and Philosophy*, 1923, second edition, 1930.

KARL MARX

"anti-authoritarian," "anti-political," and "anti-party" groups of the day. The violent battle waged by Marx and his followers against that heterodoxy led to the formal expulsion of the dissident groups from the "International" and, finally, to the dissolution of the whole organization. A direct descendant of this earliest form of an economistic and anti-political tendency is that second current of socialistic thought which was represented by revolutionary syndicalism and anarcho-syndicalism and is actually responsible for that second great rallying of the proletarian forces after the Russian Revolution of October 1917, which formed during the last seven years the real driving force of the revolutionary movement in Spain.[1] The same revolutionary economistic tendency was represented, in a weaker form, within the Marxist movement itself.

We do not mean here that pseudo-economistic school of the German and other European Social Democratic parties and Trade Unions which under the pretext of an "economistic" principle actually contested all forms of the workers' movement going beyond the mere "economic" wage struggle within the framework of the bourgeois production and of the bourgeois State. On the basis of that pseudo-economistic principle, they opposed, in the period preceding the World War, among other political activities of the workers, the Social Democratic campaign for the abolition of the property qualification on the franchise in Prussia, the militant Liebknecht campaign against militarism, and the so-called "révolution Dreyfusienne" in France. They did so not for any particular dislike of the very moderate political aims of those campaigns, but on the ground of the "revolutionary" weapons (general strikes, street demonstrations, etc.) employed therein. Thus they did not oppose politics but only the alliance of the workers with a radical bourgeois politics. They opposed on the same grounds, during the

[1] See the author's article on *The Spanish Revolution* in *Die Neue Rundschau*, Berlin, 1931.

216

war, even the slightest attempts of the socialist workers in Germany to endanger the "Burgfrieden" thrust upon them in the interest of the ruling class.

While this group emphasized the "materialistic" importance of a so-called "economic action" only for the purpose of avoiding the revolutionary implications of an unrestricted political fight, the real importance of an *economic* action in a social struggle for power was worked out, both against the pseudo-economism of the reformists and against the merely political radicalism of the party leadership, by that small revolutionary group of the German Social Democratic Party which then centred around Rosa Luxemburg. That left-wing radicalism of the pre-war period developed during the war, and the ensuing phase of a direct revolutionary struggle, into the anti-parliamentary and anti-trade union tendency of the left communists, who with several directly anarchistic and syndicalistic currents, took a considerable share in the foundation of the new international organization of the revolutionary working class to be later shoved into the background again by the increasing stabilization of the old capitalist conditions. They were then, after a vehement internal struggle, finally expelled from the ranks of the communist Third International by a process begun by Lenin himself,[1] and followed out to the bitter end by the "queue de Lenin" after his death.

As shown by this brief historical outline, the "economistic tendency" of Marxism has played, on the whole, an important part in the revolutionary development of the European labour movement comparable to the contribution which during the same period was made by the Industrial Workers of the World to the revolutionary development of the class war in the U.S.A. This was recognized even by such an arch-political Marxist as Lenin when, on looking back to his own battles against the

---

[1] See Lenin, *Radicalism, an Infantile Disease of Communism*, 1920.

217

reformist and centrist deformation of revolutionary Marxism within the German Social Democracy, he made the characteristic statement : "Anarchism is the punishment for the sins of opportunism."[1] Even from a merely theoretical viewpoint the connection of the Marxist theory with the whole of the revolutionary proletarian class war was preserved most efficiently by this "economistic" group, although the original Marxian idea of a continuous struggle waged simultaneously on all fronts of the social life was kept alive by them only in the "abstract" and almost mystical form of a direct identification of the objective economic development with the active revolutionary movement of the proletarian class.

In opposition to that first extreme stands another and apparently much more comprehensive interpretation of revolutionary Marxism which will hereafter be called the "sociological tendency." While the former school over-emphasized the importance of economics and more or less "one-sidedly" reduced all social relations and developments to the unique "reality" of material production, this other school of Marxian thought, in an equally one-sided manner, strove to supplant the basic importance of the production-relations for all political, legal, ideological phenomena occurring in a given socio-economic formation by a "co-ordination" of the "interactions" going to and fro between the various departments of social life and, ultimately, by a "universal interdependence of all social spheres." The materialistic conception of history, then, no longer appears as the principle of a materialistic science, investigating all facts of history from the point of view of their specific relation to *material production*. It appears at its best as a *general empirical and positivistic method* which represents all facts in their own contexts and not in connection with any preconceived "idea" at all. Thus the materialistic *Critique of Political*

[1] See Lenin, *Radicalism, an Infantile Disease of Communism*, 1920.

218

Economy is no longer regarded as the foundation of the whole materialistic investigation of society, but is transformed into a mere application of the general principles formulated by the materialistic conception of history to one particular section of historical data. Besides the system of materialistic economics, which has been represented in detailed form by Marx in *Capital*, there are, according to this second school, other partial systems which have not yet been fully carried out but which are theoretically equally important parts of the whole of an all-comprehensive materialistic system. There are, for example, the "materialistic" systems of politics, law, philosophy, culture, etc.[1]

Thus the economic materialism of Marx is disintegrated into a series of separate and co-ordinated "sociological" sciences and thereby stripped of all definite historical contents as well as of its distinct revolutionary character. From a radical attack upon the whole of the present-day capitalistic mode of production it is transformed into a theoretical criticism of various aspects of the existing capitalistic system as its economic organization, its State, its educational system, its religion, art, science ; a criticism which no longer necessarily leads up to a revolutionary practice, but may just as well spend itself (and actually has already spent itself) in all kinds of reforms, which nowhere surpass the bounds of the existing bourgeois society and its State.[2]

In order to restore the full theoretical and practical meaning of Marx's critical materialistic principle we start with the statement that the materialistic principle of Marx does not need any such completion of its propositions as was offered by the theory of the so-called "inter-actions." When Marx and Engels formulated their materialistic principle, they were fully aware

[1] For a more detailed discussion of this conception of Marxism see the author's *Principles of the Materialistic Conception of History*, Berlin, 1922, pp. 11 *et seq.*
[2] See the author's *Marxism and Philosophy*, p. 83.

of the fact that "the same economic basis by innumerable different empirical circumstances, natural conditions, race differences, external historical influences, etc., may appear in an unlimited range of variations and graduations which can only be understood by an analysis of those given empirical circumstances."[1] They comprised, in their investigation of the effects of the economic basis upon the superstructure, and of the social existence upon the consciousness, as a matter of course, the concrete forms in which, e.g., the master and servant relation that naturally grows from the given mode of production, afterwards reacts upon the mode of production itself. Nor have they treated the so-called "intellectual production" as a simple reflex of material production, but rather they have represented along with the existing historical forms of material production also "the definite forms of the intellectual production corresponding to that material production and their mutual connection."[2]

To gain a clearer insight into the manner in which Marx and Engels dealt with the links between the economic basis and the superstructure of a given society, it is advisable to study first the manner in which they dealt with the same connection appearing within the economic structure itself. While they described the more general aspects of their materialistic method in a half-philosophical form when historical materialism was still in the making,[3] they applied it in detail to the economic sphere in the scientific writings of their later period. It is here that they finally proved the superiority of their method of dealing with historical and social connections over that "crude and conceptless manner" in which the bourgeois economists first arbitrarily tore asunder the existing links between production, distribution, circulation, consumption, and then, by an afterthought, reunited them as though they were really independent existences and had not

[1] See *Capital*, III, ii, p. 325.
[2] See Marx, *Theories of Surplus Value*, I, pp. 381 *et seq*.
[3] See especially the extensive MSS. of the *German Ideology*, 1845-46 (MEGA, I, v, pp. 1-672).

been arbitrarily separated by theoretical reflection. They likewise opposed the insufficient form in which some philosophers, historians, and "social belletrists" had treated those various fields as directly "identical."[1]

The positive standpoint of historical materialism appears from a statement in which Marx summed up a thorough analysis of the various ways in which the different spheres of production, distribution, etc., can be said to condition each other :—"The result is not that production, distribution, exchange, consumption, etc., are identical, but that they all are 'moments' of a totality, differences within a unity. *Production encroaches over the other 'moments.'* From it the whole process begins always anew . . . It follows that a definite form of production conditions definite forms of consumption, distribution, exchange, and the definite relations prevailing between those different 'moments' themselves. It is true that *production in its narrower definition is in turn determined by other 'moments'* ; for instance, when the market expands, i.e., when the sphere of exchange enlarges, production grows in extent and subdivides within itself. Again production is affected by a change in the distribution, e.g., by a concentration of capital, by a change in the distribution of the population between town and country, etc. Finally, the needs of consumption determine production. There is an interaction between the various 'moments.' Such is the case with every organic unity."[2]

There was then, as against the manner in which the materialistic principle had been applied by its initiators themselves, no needs of that violent criticism which was at a later time directed by Friedrich Engels against the so-called "one-sidedness" of the materialistic principle.

This apparent "self-criticism" which is embodied in a series of letters written by Engels in the 90's to several younger adherents

[1] See *Introduction* 1857, pp. 714 *et seq.*
[2] *Ibid.* p. 744.

of the Marxian theory[1] and which since then has been the main source of inspiration to all revisionist and bourgeois "improvers" of Marx's revolutionary materialistic principle, was in truth directed against a too dogmatic and abstract interpretation of historical materialism, which had then arisen in the writings of some of the younger of its most ardent supporters, e.g., in the "*Lessing Legend*" of Franz Mehring.[2]

There is no doubt that here as in many other cases, Engels overstated his own and Marx's responsibility for the mistakes committed by their followers, when he declared that "at first we all have neglected the formal aspect too much in favour of the contents."[3] He thus unintentionally supported that other school of the younger generation of Marxists who under the cover of an attack on a too simple and "vulgar" interpretation of Marx's materialism really aimed at depriving the new doctrine of its revolutionary implications in order to make it acceptable to the bourgeoisie. It was just the struggle waged by that new Marxist school in the theoretical arena against Mehring's somewhat abstract presentment of Marx's materialism, that opened the way for the new "revisionistic" tendency which was later to get the upper hand in the German Marxist party and trade union movement and to lead it through the events of 1914 to 1918 to its complete annihilation in 1933.

[1] See *Dokumente des Sozialismus*, vol. II, 1903, and for an English translation Sidney Hook, *Towards the understanding of Karl Marx*, 1933, Appendix 1-3. The addressees were either people who like the Sombart student, Walter Borgius (Heinz Starkenburg), had never really endorsed the revolutionary implications of Marxism or, like Conrad Schmidt and J. Bloch, from apparently hopeful pupils of Marxism developed in a very short time to theoretical exponents of the revisionistic wing of the German social democratic party. The historical function performed by these letters in the later development was foreshadowed by the fact that they were first published in 1903, amidst the famous debate on the "revisionistic" issue and, in fact, by the leading initiator of revisionism, Eduard Bernstein, himself.

[2] See *Neue Zeit*, X, i (1892), pp. 540 *et seq.*

[3] See the section of Engels' letter of 14.7.1893 reproduced by Mehring in the notes added to the 1st vol. of his *History of German Social Democracy* (English translation by Hook l.c. Appendix 4).

The assumed one-sidedness of the Marxian materialistic conception of history exists in truth only in its abstract formulation. A theoretical statement of the connections between the economic, political, juridical, and intellectual structure of a given society unavoidably generalizes, to a certain extent, the definite historical facts, from which it is derived and to which it is to be applied as a working principle by the scientific investigator and by the practical politician. They are indeed "one-sided" as compared with the imaginary "completeness" of the actual historical "experience" or, for that matter, with the mere copying of reality which is the aim of a purely descriptive historical science, or with that "concrete" reproduction of the real which may be achieved by an artistic representation. But that "one-sidedness" is only another name for the generality of the scientific form. One might as well complain of the "one-sidedness" of the physicists who subject the many different kinds of movement of inanimate and animate bodies to the law of gravity, without taking into account the "modifications" brought about by secondary conditions. Just as with the laws of physics and technology, the apparent "one-sidedness" adhering to the "laws" of social being, historical development, and practical action as formulated by Marx, in no way interferes with their practical and theoretical utility, nay more, that utility depends upon the "one-sidedness" of their theoretical formulation.

The "watering" process applied to the materialistic scheme by the Marxist "sociologists" does not therefore so much correct a faulty "one-sidedness" as it impairs the scientific utility of the scheme itself. The doctrine of an indifferent play of "actions" and "interactions," or of the general "interdependence of the social spheres" does not give us the slightest hint whether we should seek for the cause of a change occurring in any definite sector of social life—and thus also for the practical means of bringing about a change of the conditions existing in that sector —in the "action" of the basis on the superstructure or in the

223

"reaction" of the superstructure on the basis. Nor is that want of definiteness supplanted by describing in unprecise terms the economic basis as a "primary," and the superstructure as a "secondary," factor of the historical development, or by referring to the economic conditions as the "finally decisive moment." No scientist can be contented with the answer given by Engels to one of his correspondents, in which he said that, of all the conditions that form the given "environment" for human actions, "the economic conditions, however much they may be influenced themselves by conditions of a political and ideological order, are still in the last instance the decisive ones, forming the red thread which runs through the whole and alone leads to a real understanding."[1]

All these phrases are but useless attempts to adhere to the "dialectical" unity of substance, causality, and interaction in the Hegelian philosophical "idea",[2] as against an altogether changed mode of thought prevailing during the second half of the 19th century. When that first generation of Marxist theorists who had been through the school of Hegel, or that new generation of Marxist Hegelians who have arisen in Russia since the 90's, were confronted with the question originating from quite a different general attitude and tradition of thought :—"In what sense are economic conditions *causal* (as sufficient reason ? occasion ? permanent condition, etc. ?) to development ?"[3] their first reaction was a flood of protests against this new generation which had fallen so low that it no longer understood anything about that ars magna—Dialectics. Said Engels :—"What all these gentlemen lack, is dialectics. They never see anything but here cause and there effect. That this is an empty abstraction, that such metaphysical polar opposites exist in the real world only in time of crisis, while the whole vast process moves in the

[1] See Engels' letter to Starkenburg, 25.1.1894.
[2] See Hegel, *Encyclopædia*, §§ 142-59.
[3] This was the first of the two questions addressed to Engels by Borgius (Starkenburg), the pupil of Sombart, and answered in the letter of 25.1.1894

form of interactions, although of very unequal forces among which the economic movement is by far the strongest, the most original, and the most decisive ; that here nothing is absolute and everything is relative, this they never begin to see ; for them there has been no Hegel."[1] In all that semi-defence of Hegelian philosophy, they were nevertheless unable to save from Hegel's dialectical "idea" more than that one meagre concept of "inter-action" which for Hegel had been closely connected with other concepts in the unity of a truly philosophical thought. Thus they succeeded only in adding to the abstract scientific form of causality another scientific term equally abstract, though not at all equally well-defined.[2] This was not Hegel's philosophical concept, but merely that "abstract" concept which had been described by him contemptuously as a mere "refuge of reflection," and a "poor category" which was no longer sufficient for the "observation of nature and of the living organism," let alone for "historical observation." "If we consider, e.g., the customs of the Spartans as the effect of their constitution and thus, contrarywise, the latter as the effect of their customs, no matter how correct such a statement otherwise may be, yet this view will never give us final satisfaction because in truth neither the constitution nor the customs of that people are grasped in it."[3]

Hence those "interactions" which were supposed to preserve within the materialistic scheme of Marxism the philosophical dialectics of Hegel are neither fish nor fowl nor good red herring, they are neither Hegelian philosophy, mystically vague yet full of matter, nor are they scientific terms precisely defined

[1] See Engels' letter to Conrad Schmidt of 27.10.1890. A similar attitude was adopted as late as 1914 by Lenin when he put into his notebook the following "Aphorism" :—One cannot fully understand Marx's Capital, and particularly the first chapter unless one has thoroughly studied and grasped the whole of Hegel's Logic. Thus it is that after half a century none of the Marxists have understood Marx!" (See Extracts and Marginal Notes on Hegel's Science of Logic—Marx-Engels-Lenin-Institute, Moscow, 1932, p. 99).
[2] See the author's Marxism and Philosophy, p. 98, footnote 56.
[3] See Hegel, Encyclopædia, addition to § 156.

225

on the model of modern physics. As long as there is no sufficiently exact determination of the quantitative amount of action and reaction and of the precise conditions under which at a given time the one or the other will take place, the original statement of the materialistic principle will be in no way clarified or improved by the super-addition of so-called "interactions" which are deemed to be at one and the same time co-ordinate and subordinate to the original "causes." It is, on the contrary, deprived of all precise meaning by that utterly meaningless addition and thus transformed into a scientifically useless phrase.

There is much more to be said about the peculiar quality of "one-sidedness" attached to every great revolutionary epoch-making theory. Already the earlier form of the "milieu" theory advanced by bourgeois materialists and worked out more consistently by Robert Owen in his system of communism, owed its progressive importance to that very one-sidedness which of the manifold factors in historical development stressed just the one—and the one only—which until then had been entirely neglected. It loses all importance and even the semblance of originality and depth which gives a certain flashy appearance even to the caricatured form which it subsequently assumed in Taine's belated indictment of the bourgeois revolution of the 18th century, if it is enlarged to the "impartial" statement that man is, indeed, on the one hand a product of his conditions but on the other hand is, conversely, also the cause or the "producer" of his own conditions of existence. Even more superfluous and damaging are such "supplements" to the historical and social materialism which has been developed from the "milieu" theory of early bourgeois materialism by Marx. His statement that "property relations are a juridical expression of existing production-relations" was transformed into a hackneyed commonplace by that modern German philosopher who concluded that, though on the one hand all law is to be considered as a mere form of the economic contents, on the other hand economic phenomena must themselves be understood as mere "mass-phenomena of legal relations" and thus both are to be inter-changeably explained by each other.[1]

Neither "dialectical causality" in its philosophical definition, nor scientific "causality" supplemented by "interactions," is sufficient to determine the particular kinds of connections and relations existing between the economic "basis" and the juridical, political, and ideological "superstructure" of a given socio-economic formation. Twentieth century natural science is aware that the "causal" relations occurring in a particular field of knowledge are not to be defined by a general concept or "law" of causality, but must be determined specifically for each separate sphere.[2] The most important pioneer work for the establishment of the same scientific principle in the sphere of the historical, social, and practical life of man was done in a philosophical form by the dialectics of Hegel and continued in a form, no longer philosophical and yet not entirely separated from the Hegelian philosophy, by the materialistic dialectics of Marx and Engels. The greater part of the results thus obtained do not consist in theoretical formulæ, but in the specific application of the new principle to a number of questions which are either of funda-mental practical importance or of an extremely subtle nature theoretically, and which had not, up to that time, been so much as touched by other investigators.[3] Even in the future the main

---

[1] See R. Stammler, *Economics and Law According to the Materialistic Conception of History*, 1896.

[2] See Philipp Frank, *The Law of Causality and its Limits*, Vienna, 1932.

[3] Here belong, e.g., the questions dealing with the "uneven develop-ment" of various spheres of social life, enumerated by Marx *Introduction*, 1857, pp. 779 *et seq.*: uneven development of material and artistic produc-tion (and of the various forms of art among themselves) ; formation-process of U.S.A. as compared with that of Europe; uneven development of production-relations in form of legal relations, etc. Here belong, further-more, Lenin's law of the "uneven development of capitalism in different countries", the "law of combined development" discussed by Trotzky in the first chapter of his *History of the Russian Revolution* (1931); the law of the "lag of the ideological development" as formulated by Varga and other Marxian writers, etc.

task of scientific research in this field will not lie in the theoretical statement of any new formulæ. To a great extent, the new results will come from a further application and testing of the principles implicit in Marx. Nor should we adhere too strictly to the words of Marx who often used his terms only figuratively as, for instance, in describing the connections here considered as a relation between "basis" and "superstructure," as a "correspondence," etc. He presented the history of society at one time as a development of material productive powers and production-relations ; at another time, as a history of the class struggle. In the same broad way, he used the terms of "basis" and "superstructure" applying them on one occasion to production-relations and such institutional phenomena as "State" and "law" and, on another occasion, to the proletariat and the "higher" strata of official society borne by that lower stratum and to be rent asunder by its upheaval.[1] There is no need to smooth over such apparent contradictions by a scholastic interpretation ; to say, e.g., that the organization of the workers as a social class rests on the economic conditions of a given epoch but that, at the same time, the further historical development of the economic conditions is influenced by the class struggle or, conversely, that the class struggle develops under the stimulus of the productive forces but determines, within a given period, the existing economic conditions. By the former interpretation, the term of the "productive forces," by the latter, the concept of the "class struggle" is deprived of what was with Marx their main content. While these terms may be applied also to a mere description of a given historical state of society they both attain their full and true significance only when applied to the genetic and revolutionary process by which each given form is transformed into a new and higher form of development.

As a matter of fact, the "objective" description of the historical process as a development of the productive forces and the "sub-

[1] See *Preface* 1859 and *Communist Manifesto* (MEGA, I, vi, p. 536).

jective" description of history as a class struggle are two independent forms of Marxian thought, equally original and not derived one from the other, which are worked out in an objective and simultaneously subjective materialistic theory for the use of the investigator and which, at the same time, are meant to be applied by the proletarian class in its practical struggle. In either case, they are to be applied singly or together, according to the conditions of each given position, as an instrument for the most precise solution of the task in hand. The Marxian concepts (as among the later Marxists was most clearly realized by Sorel and Lenin[1]) are not new dogmatic fetters or pre-established points which must be gone through in a particular order in any "materialistic" investigation. They are an undogmatic guide for scientific research and revolutionary action. "The proof of the pudding is in the eating."

[1] See G. Sorel, *Introduction à l'économie moderne*, 3-me edition 1919, pp. 386 *et seq.* For the earliest form of Lenin's criticism of "objective" Marxism see the pamphlet, *The Economic Content of Narodnikidom and its Critique in Mr. Struve's Book*, 1895; for his last years, the critical comments on N. Suchannovs Notes *On Our Revolution*, 1923 (Collected Works I and XXVII—Russian).

CHAPTER VII

CONCLUSIONS

MARX'S most important contributions to social research are that he :

(1) related all phenomena of the life process of society to economics ;

(2) conceived of economics itself as a social science ;

(3) defined all social phenomena historically and, indeed, as a revolutionary process which results from the development of the material forces of production and is realized by the struggle of the social classes.

These three general results of the Marxian science of society include as particularly important partial results :

(4) an exact definition of the relation between economics and politics ;

(5) a reduction of all phenomena of the so-called "mind" to definite forms of social consciousness pertaining to a definite historical epoch.

A detailed analysis of topics (4) and (5) is beyond the scope of this work.

To arrive at these results, Marx used a conceptual framework of his own, which he composed largely of philosophical elements reshaped from Hegel, but into which he absorbed as well all the new tendencies of the social knowledge of his time. In conscious opposition to Hegel's idealistic system, he called this new set of ideas his *materialism*. As against the various other materialistic tenets, he described it more precisely by the addition of one or more such adjectives as historical, dialectical, critical, revolutionary, scientific, or proletarian.

Historical materialism is in its main tendency no longer a philosophical, but rather an empirical and scientific, method.

It contains the premises for a real solution of the task which naturalistic materialism and positivism had only apparently solved by an eclectic application to the science of society of the highly specialized methods which, through centuries of study, the natural scientists had invented and meticulously adapted to their particular fields of investigation. Instead of transferring those scientific methods ready-made to the new sphere of society, Marx developed specific methods of social research, a *Novum Organum* which would permit the investigator in this newly opened field to penetrate the "*eidola*" standing in the way of unbiassed research, and to determine "with the precision of natural science" the real subject-matter hidden behind an interminable confusion of "ideological" disguises. This is the kernel of Marxian materialism.

Just as positivism could not move with freedom in the new field of social science, but remained tied to the specific concepts and methods of natural science, so Marx's historical materialism has not entirely freed itself from the spell of Hegel's philosophical method which in its day overshadowed all contemporary thought. This was not a materialistic science of society which had developed on its own basis. Rather it was a materialistic theory that had just emerged from idealistic philosophy ; a theory, therefore, which still showed in its contents, its methods, and its terminology the birth-marks of the old Hegelian philosophy from whose womb it sprang. All these imperfections were unavoidable under the circumstances out of which Marx's materialistic social research arose. With all these faults, it was far and away in advance of the other contemporary schools of social thought. It remains superior to all other social theories even now, in spite of the comparatively negligible progress which Marxists have in the meantime made in the formal development of the methods discovered by Marx and Engels. In a partly philosophical form, it has yet achieved a great number of important scientific results which hold good to this day.

Through Hegel, the new proletarian materialism linked itself to the sum of bourgeois social thought of the preceding historical period. It did so in the same antagonistic manner in which, during the same period, the historical movement of the bourgeoisie was continued by the new revolutionary movement of the proletarian class.

The philosophical idealism of Hegel corresponded to a further advanced stage of the material development of society than did the old bourgeois materialism. Hegel had embodied in his "idealistic" system a greater number of elements that could be used by the new historical materialism. He had also presented them in a more highly developed form than had any of the 18th century materialists.[1] We have seen in a former chapter how loosely Hegel's doctrine of "civil society" was connected with the whole of his idealistic system.[2] Similarly, many other sections of Hegel's system can without difficulty be read materialistically instead of idealistically.

The fact that the new proletarian theory had incorporated in its methods and contents some important results of Hegel's philosophy, did not in any way infer an obligation. Marx and Engels disrupted the elements which in Hegel had been bound up in an idealistic system. They welded together the parts which they found suitable for their purpose, with elements taken from other sources into the new whole of a materialistic science.

Hegel had been in his time an encyclopædic thinker, a genius at annexation, a "philosopher" hungry both for theory and reality, who brought within the scope of his system an incomparably greater field of experience than anyone since Aristotle. The mass

[1] In the same sense Lenin noted in 1914, on reading Hegel's *Philosophy of History*: "Intelligent idealism is nearer intelligent materialism than is unintelligent materialism." The "unintelligent" materialism is the undeveloped early bourgeois materialism in contrast to the "intelligent" idealism of Hegel and the intelligent materialism of Marx. (See Extracts and Marginal Notes on Hegel's *Philosophy of History*—Marx-Engels-Lenin-Institute, Moscow 1932, p. 212).

[2] See above, pp. 20 *et seq.*

of thought-material stored up in Hegel's philosophy is, never-theless, only one of the tributaries which Marx and Engels directed into the broad stream of their new materialistic doctrine of society. They took from all sides. From the bourgeois historians of the French Restoration they took the historical import-ance of class and class struggle ; from Ricardo, the conflicting economic interests of the social classes ; from Proudhon, the description of the modern proletariat as the only revolutionary class ; from the feudal and Christian assailants of the new political order born of the 18th century revolution, the ruthless unmasking of the liberal ideas of the bourgeoisie, the piercing invective full of hatred. Their ingenuous dissection of the un-solvable antagonisms of the modern mode of production they took from the petty-bourgeoisie socialism of Sismondi ; the accents of humanism perceptible even in their later materialistic writings from earlier companions among the left Hegelians, especially from Feuerbach ; the relevance of politics to the struggle of the working class from the contemporary labour parties, French Social Democrats and English Chartists ; the doctrine of the revolutionary dictatorship from the French Convention, and from Blanqui and his followers.[1] Finally, they

---

[1] See the first article of the Statement of Principles issued in 1850 by the *Société universelle des communistes révolutionnaires* (signed by the Blanquists, J. Vidil and Adam; by the communists, Willich, Marx, and Engels, by the Chartist, G. Julian Harney) which binds the associated groups, among them Marx's "Bund der Kommunisten", to the Blanquist slogans of the "permanent revolution" and the "dictatorship of the proletariat." The documents dealing with this shortlived rally of the militant extremists of the defeated 1848 revolution in a new international organisation which was soon afterwards entirely abandoned by Marx and Engels, were first published in 1928 by Rjazanov in the Russian *Bulletin of the Marx-Engels Institute* in Moscow and in the German periodical *Unter dem Banner des Marxismus*, vol. II, No. 1-2. For a reflection of this secret deal with the Blanquists in Marx's published writings of the same period, see Marx's article in *Neue Rheinische Zeitung, politisch-oekonomische Revue*, No. 3, March, 1850 (reprinted by Engels 1895 in *Klassenkaempfe in Frankreich 1848-1850*) and the circular letter to its members from the Central Committee of the reconstituted Communist League, June 1850 (printed as an *Appendix* to the Zurich edition 1885 of Marx's *Disclosures on the Communist Trial at Cologne*, 1852).

took from St. Simon, Fourier, and Owen the ultimate goal of all socialism and communism, the complete overthrow of existing capitalistic society, abolition of all classes and class oppositions, and transformation of the political State into a mere management of production. These were the annexations they had made from the beginning. During the further development of their theory, they made others, adopting, for instance, at one stroke the results of that first age of discovery in primæval research which began early in the 19th century and concluded with Morgan.

Just as Marx's new science is in its form above all a strictly empirical investigation and critique of society, so in its content it is, above all, economic research. Marx, who had begun his materialistic investigation of society as a critic of religion, of philosophy, of politics, and of law, later concentrated more and more upon economics. He did not thereby narrow down the realm of his all-comprehensive social science. The critique of Political Economy as embodied in *Capital* deals with the State and the law, and with such "higher," i.e., still more ideological, social phenomena as philosophy, art, and religion only in occasional remarks which light up, in sudden flashes, extensive fields of social activity ; yet it remains a materialistic investigation into *the whole of existing bourgeois society*. It proceeds methodically from the view that when we have examined the bourgeois mode of production and its historical changes we have thereby examined everything of the structure and development of present-day society which can be the subject-matter of a strictly empirical science. In this sense, Marx's materialistic social science is not sociology, but economics.

For the other branches of the so-called social science there remains then, according to the materialistic principle of Marxism, a scale of phenomena which become in proportion to their increasing distance from the economic foundation, less and less accessible to a strictly scientific investigation, less and less "material," more and more "ideological," and which, finally, cannot be treated in a theoretical manner at all, but only critically and in the closest connection with the practical tasks of the revolutionary class war.

The last foundation of the new Marxian science is neither Hegel nor Ricardo, neither bourgeois philosophy nor bourgeois economy. Marx's materialistic investigation into the movement of modern bourgeois society received its decisive impulses from the reality of historical development, that is, from the great bourgeois revolutions of the 17th and 18th centuries and from the historical movement of the 19th century, the revolutionary rise of the proletarian class. A genetic presentation would show with what precision and at the same time with what weight every new phase of the real history of society, every new experience of the proletarian class struggle, is reflected in each new turn of the theoretical development of Marx's doctrine. This close connection between the real history of society and Marx's materialistic science does not rest upon a mere passive reflection of reality in theory. What Marx and Engels gained in theoretical views and concepts from their study of the real history of the proletarian movement, they gave back immediately in the form of direct participation in the class conflicts of their time and of powerful impulses which historically continue to enlarge and stimulate the proletarian movement up to the present day.

To be instrumental in the historical movement of our time is the great purpose of Marx. This revolutionary principle which shapes all his later theoretical work he had formulated in his earliest youth when he concluded his violent criticism of Feuerbach's politically insufficient materialistic philosophy with a last mighty hammer stroke : "Philosophers have only interpreted the world differently ; the important thing, however, is *to change it.*"

235

BIBLIOGRAPHY

THE writings of Marx and Engels until 1848 and the complete correspondence between Marx and Engels, 1844-1883, are quoted from the Collected Works published under the auspices of the Marx-Engels-Lenin-Institute in Moscow : Marx-Engels-Gesamt-Ausgabe (MEGA), pt. I, vols. I-II and pt. III, vols. I-III, edited by D. Rjazanov, Berlin, 1927-30 ; pt. I, vols. III-VI and pt. III, vol. IV, edited by V. Adoratskij, Berlin, 1931-32. For the most complete and authentic information about their later writings see, as to Marx, the Bio-Bibliography of the same Institute : Karl Marx, Chronik seines Lebens in Einzeldaten, Moskau, 1934 ; as to Engels, Quellen und Nachweise, annexed to Gustav Mayer, Friedrich Engels, Eine Biographie in zwei Bänden, Berlin, 1933, vol. I, pp. 373-393, vol. II, pp. 535-570. All writings of Marx and Engels not included in the hitherto published volumes of MEGA, are quoted from the first editions and, in the case of unpublished MSS., documents, etc., each item in the form in which it was first printed.

WORKS OF MARX[1]

MEGA, I, i, 1 :

1. Differenz der demokritischen und epikureischen Natur-philosophie (Doktordissertation), 1841.
   The Difference between Democritean and Epicurean Philosophy of Nature.

2. Das philosophische Manifest der historischen Rechtsschule (Rheinische Zeitung, 1842, Nr. 221, Beiblatt).
   The Philosophical Manifesto of the Historical School of Law.

[1]Co-authorship of Engels is indicated by a cross printed on the margin.

3. Die Verhandlungen des 6. rheinischen Landtags. Debatten
   über das Holzdiebstahlsgesetz (Rh. Z. 1842, Nr. 298,
   Beiblatt und Nr. 307, Beiblatt).
   On the Debates of the 6th Rhineland Diet.

4. Zur Kritik der Hegelschen Rechtsphilosophie (MSS. 1843).
   Quoted as MSS. of 1843.

5. Ein Briefwechsel von 1843 (Deutsch-Französische Jahrbücher, 1844). Correspondence of 1843.

6. Einleitung zur Kritik der Hegelschen Rechtsphilosophie
   (Deutsch-Französische Jahrbücher, Paris, 1844).
   Introduction to a Critique of the Hegelian Philosophy of
   Law.

MEGA, I, i, 2 :

7. Letter to his father of 10.11.1837.

8. Letter to Ruge of 25.1.1843.

9. Letter to Ruge of 5.3.1843.

MEGA, I, iii :

10. Kritische Randglossen zu dem Artikel : "Der König
    von Preussen und die Sozialreform. Von einem
    Preussen." (Vorwärts, Pariser Deutsche Zeitschrift,
    1844.)
    Marginal Notes to Ruge's Article, "The King of Prussia
    and Social Reform."

11. Aus den Excerptenheften : über Smith ; über Mill
    (MSS., 1844). Quoted as Notes of 1844.

12. Zur Kritik der Nationaloekonomie, mit einem Schluss-
    kapitel über die Hegelsche Philosophie (Oekono-
    misch-philosophische MSS., 1844).
    Towards a Critique of National Economy (Economico-
    Philosophical MSS., 1844).

13. +Die heilige Familie, oder Kritik der kritischen Kritik.
    Gegen Bruno Bauer & Consorten. Frankfurt, 1845.
    Quoted as Holy Family, 1845.

MEGA, I, v :

14. +Die deutsche Ideologie. Kritik der neuesten deutschen Philosophie, in ihren Repräsentanten, Feuerbach, B. Bauer und Stirner, und des deutschen Sozialismus in seinen verschiedenen Propheten. (MSS., 1845-46.) The German Ideology : Critique of the New German Philosophy as represented by Feuerbach, B. Bauer, and Stirner, and of German Socialism and its various Prophets. Quoted as *German Ideology*, 1845-46.

15. Thesen Ueber Feuerbach (MSS., 1845 ; first published by Engels as Appendix to No. 51 below). Quoted as *Theses on Feuerbach*, 1845.

MEGA, I, vi :

16. Misère de la philosophie. Réponse à la philosophie de la misère de M. Proudhon. Paris - Bruxelles, 1847. Quoted as *Anti-Proudhon*, 1847.

17. Arbeitslohn (MSS., 1847 ; later published in a revised form under different title, see No. 18).

18. Lohnarbeit und Kapital (Neue Rheinische Zeitung, 1849, No. 264 et seq., 5.4.–11.4). Wage-Labour and Capital.

19. Leitartikel der Neuen Rheinischen Zeitung, 4.4.1849. Leading Article of Neue Rheinische Zeitung. Nos. 18 and 19 re-edited with an introduction by Engels under heading, "Lohnarbeit und Kapital" (1891).

20. Aus den Excerptenheften : über Quesnay ; über Brissot (MSS., 1845-46). Quoted as *Notes of 1845-46*.

21. +Manifest der Kommunistischen Partei. London, 1848. Manifesto of the Communist Party. Quoted as *Communist Manifesto*, 1848.

22. Ansprache der Zentralbehörde des Bundes der Kommunisten, Juni, 1850 (printed as an Appendix to the Zurich edition, 1852, of No. 26 below).

239

Circular Letter to its Members from the Central Committee of the Communist League, June, 1850.

23. Neue Rheinische Zeitung, politisch-ökonomische Revue. Heft 3 ; März, 1850.

24. +Doppelheft, 5/6 ; November, 1850.
Nos. 23 and 24 re-edited with an introduction by Engels under heading "Die Klassenkämpfe in Frankreich, 1848-50," 1895.

25. Der 18. Brumaire des Louis Napoleon (Die Revolution, Eine Zeitschrift in zwanglosen Heften, New York, 1852 ; reprinted in book form, Hamburg, 1869).
The 18th Brumaire of Louis Bonaparte, 1852.

26. Enthüllungen über den Kommunistenprozess zu Köln, 1852.
Disclosures on the Communist Trial at Cologne, 1852.

27. Einleitung zur Kritik der Politischen Oekonomie (MSS., 1857 ; printed Neue Zeit XXI, 1, 1903). Quoted as *Introduction* 1857.

28. Vorwort zur Kritik der Politischen Oekonomie, 1859. Quoted as *Preface* 1859.

29. Zur Kritik der Politischen Oekonomie (Heft 1, Berlin, 1857). Quoted as *Critique of Political Economy*, 1859.

30. Vorwort zur 1. Auflage des Kapital, 1867.
Preface to 1st edition of Capital, 1867.

31. Nachwort zur 2. Auflage des Kapital, 1872. Quoted as *Postscript* 1873.

32. Das Kapital, Buch I : Der Produktionsprozess des Kapitals ; 1. Auflage, 1867; 2. Auflage, 1872, 3. Auflage, edited by Fr. Engels, 1883 (quoted from the 4th edition, edited by Fr. Engels, Hamburg, 1890).

33. +Das Kapital, Buch II : Der Zirkulationsprozess des Kapitals, edited by Engels, Hamburg, 1885.

34. +Das Kapital, Buch III : Der Gesamtprozess der kapitalistischen Produktion, edited by Engels, Hamburg, 1894.

35. Vorarbeiten zur Kritik der Politischen Oekonomie, Heft 6-15 (MSS., 1861-63, edited by Kautsky under the heading "Theorien über den Mehrwert," vols. I-III, Stuttgart, 1905-10). Quoted as *Theories on Surplus Value*.

36. Address and Provisional Rules of the Working Men's International Association (printed at the Beehive Newspaper Office, London, 1864).

37. Schreiben vom 24.1.1865, über P. J. Proudhon (Sozial-demokrat, Berlin, 1865, Nr. 16-18).
Letter to the Editor of the Sozialdemokrat, 24.1.1865.

38. Randglossen zum Programm der Deutschen Arbeiter-partei (MS., 1875, printed Neue Zeit IX, 1, 1891).
Marginal Notes to the Programme of the German Labour Party, 1875.

39. Entwurf einer Entgegnung auf Michaelovskys Aufsatz in Otetshestvennye Sapiski, Petersburg, 1877, Heft 10 (MS., 1877 ; first published in Russian in Viestnik Narodnoy Voli, 1866 ; German translation in Sozial-demokrat, Zurich, 1887, and in Volkszeitung, New York, 1887).
Letter to the Editor of Otetshestvennye Sapiski, 1877.

40. Oekonomisches en général (MSS. of 1881-82, printed as *Appendix* to the 1932 edition of *Capital*, by the Marx-Engels-Lenin-Institute in Moscow).

WORKS OF ENGELS

41. Umrisse zu einer Kritik der Nationaloekonomie (Deutsch-Französische Jahrbücher, Paris, 1844 ; reprinted MEGA, I, ii).
Outlines of a Critique of National Economy, 1844.

42. Rezension von Nr. 29 (Das Volk, London, 1859).
Review of Marx's Critique of Political Economy, 1859.

43. Dell'Autorità (Pubblicazione della Plebe, Lodi, 1873).

44. Herrn Eugen Dührings Umwälzung der Wissenschaft
(Vorwärts, Leipzig, 1877 ; reprinted in book form
under the same title, 1878). Quoted as *Anti-Dühring*,
1878.

45. Socialisme utopique et socialisme scientifique, Paris, 1880
(revised edition in pamphlet form of No. 44 ; German
edition under heading "Die Entwicklung des Sozialismus von der Utopie zur Wissenschaft," 1883).
Quoted as *Socialism, Utopian* and *Scientific*.

46. Speech at the funeral of Marx, 17.3.1883 (printed in
German in the Sozialdemokrat, Zurich, 22.3.1883).

47. Der Ursprung der Familie, des Privateigentums und des
Staats, 1884.
Origin of the Family, Private Property, and the State,
1884.

48. How not to translate Marx (The Commonwealth, London,
November, 1885).

49. Preface to first German edition of No. 16, 1884.

50. Preface to No. 33, 1885.

51. Ludwig Feuerbach und der Ausgang der klassischen Philosophie, 1888. Quoted as *On Feuerbach*, 1888.

52. Preface to Nos. 18/19, 1891.

53. Preface to No. 34, 1894.

54. Preface to Nos. 23/24, 1895.

55. Briefe über materialistische Geschichtsauffassung, 1889-
94 (printed in Dokumente des Sozialismus, vol. II,
1903, and in Mehring, Geschichte der deutschen
Sozialdemokratie, 2nd ed. 1903).
Letters on the Materialistic Conception of History, 1889-
94 (English translation in Appendixes 1-4 of Sidney
Hook, Towards The Understanding of Karl Marx,
London-New York, 1933).

CORRESPONDENCE

56.	Marx to Engels	14. 6.1853	MEGA, III, i
57.		2. 4.1858	III, ii
58.		29.11.1858	III, ii
59.		7. 7.1866	III, iii
60.		12.12.1866	III, iii
61.		24. 4.1867	III, iii
62.		27. 7.1867	III, iii
63.		24. 8.1867	III, iii
64.		8. 1.1868	III, iv
65.		25. 3.1868	III, iv
66.		30. 4.1868	III, iv
67.		23. 5.1868	III, iv
68.	Engels to Marx	19.11.1844	III, i
69.		19. 8.1846	III, i
70.		middle of October, 1846	III, i

71. Marx to Annenkov 28.12.1846 (Mouvement Socialiste, vol. 33, Paris, 1913).
72. Marx to Weydemeyer   5. 3.1852
73. Marx to Kugelmann   11. 7.1868
74. Marx to Kugelmann   27. 6.1870
75. Marx to Beesly   12. 6.1871
76. Engels to F. A. Lange   11. 3.1865
77. Engels to Bernstein   23. 5.1884
78. Engels to Toennies   24. 1.1895

Writings of the Author quoted in this book.

79. Kernpunkte der materialistischen Geschichtsauffassung, Berlin, 1922.
    Principles of the Materialistic Conception of History, 1922.
80. Arbeitsrecht für Betriebsräte, Berlin, 1922.
    The Law of Labour. For the Use of Workers' Committees, Shop Stewards, Trade Unionists, etc., 1922.

81. Marximus und Philosophie, 1st edition, Leipzig, 1923, 2nd edition, Leipzig, 1930.
    Marxism and Philosophy, 1923/30.
82. Die materialistische Geschichtsauffassung. Eine Auseinandersetzung mit Karl Kautsky, Leipzig, 1929.
    The Materialistic Conception of History. A Critical Examination of the Work of Karl Kautsky, 1929.
83. Die spanische Revolution (Neue Rundschau, Berlin, 1931).
84. Thesen über Hegel und die Revolution—published on the 100th anniversary of Hegel's death (1931) in German and French periodicals ; most available in La Critique Sociale No. 5, Paris, 1932.
85. Geleitwort zur Volksausgabe des Kapital ; ungekürzte Ausgabe nach der 2. Auflage von 1872, G. Kiepenheuer Verlag und Verlag des Allgemeinen Deutschen Gewerkschaftsbundes, Berlin, 1932.
    Introduction to Popular Edition of Capital, 1932.
86. Werner Sombart (Grünberg's Archiv zur Geschichte des Sozialismus und der Arbeiterbewegung, Vol. XVI, 1931).
87. Karl Marx (Encyclopædia of the Social Sciences, Vol. 10, 1933).
88. Why I am a Marxist (Modern Monthly, New York, April, 1935).

INDEX OF NAMES

245